Exploring infertility issues in adoption

Ian Millar and
Christina Paulson-Ellis

BAAF
ADOPTION
& FOSTERING

Published by
**British Association for Adoption & Fostering
(BAAF)**
Saffron House
6–10 Kirby Street
London EC1N 8TS
www.baaf.org.uk

Charity Registration 275689 (England and Wales) and
SC039337 (Scotland)

British Library Cataloguing in Publication Data
A catalogue record for this book is available from the
British Library

ISBN 978 1 905664 44 3

Project management by Jo Francis, BAAF
Photograph on cover posed by models
by www.istockphoto.com
Typeset by Avon DataSet Ltd, Bidford on Avon,
Warwickshire
Printed in Great Britain by Athenaeum Press
Trade distribution by Turnaround Publisher Services,
Unit 3, Olympia Trading Estate, Coburg Road,
London N22 6TZ

BAAF is the leading UK-wide membership organisation
for all those concerned with adoption, fostering and
child care issues.

Contents

Acknowledgements

Many people offered considerable assistance and support in the production of this guide and are due our gratitude.

Jackie Quick of Norfolk County Council shared valuable thinking and experience around working with infertile adopters, as did Anne McAfee and Maureen Kinnell of the Scottish Adoption Association. Clare Brown of Infertility Network UK provided much useful information on resources and Isobel O'Neill, infertility counsellor at Glasgow Royal Infirmary, gave real insights into the far-reaching implications and emotional impact of infertility. Dr Helen Palmer, Consultant Community Paediatrician, Gateshead NHS Foundation Trust, scrutinised the medical content of the publication and very constructive comments on initial draft texts came from Mary Francis of Medway Council. We are especially grateful to "Susan and Andrew", who kindly allowed us to use the diary they wrote as part of their adoption application, permitting us a glimpse of the emotional and physical journey they undertook together. The readers of the final manuscript gave us pertinent suggestions which enabled us to refine the text and Alexandra Plumtree, Legal Adviser, BAAF Scotland, provided legal scrutiny. To these and the many others who offered help, we are extremely grateful.

Note about the authors

Ian Millar has worked almost exclusively in the field of adoption and fostering in both Scotland and England, since qualifying as a social worker in 1973. He has recently retired after 12 years in the post of Social Work Consultant/Trainer, BAAF Scotland.

Christina Paulson-Ellis spent the major part of her social work career working in adoption and fostering. Her final post was Team Leader at Norfolk County Council's Adoption and Family Finding Unit. Since retirement, she has continued a voluntary involvement with adoption through BAAF Scotland and the Scottish Adoption Association. She is an adoptive parent.

Introduction

Introduction

Rachel Black, co-author of *Beyond Childlessness*, raises the fundamental question of why people find the subject of infertility so difficult to talk about, 'other than flippantly, vaguely or not at all' (Black and Scull, 2005, p. 12). Arguably, the one time this taboo is breached outside a medical context is during an assessment to become an adoptive parent. The adoption assessment process contains several elements: the gathering of information; checking, verifying and screening; education and preparation; evaluation and analysis. It must also be a dynamic, interactive process which allows applicants to reflect on their life experiences, to understand their values, beliefs and feelings, to consider the impact adoption will have on their lives forever and to contemplate the changes and compromises which will be necessary. Infertility is one of life's major events and must be closely considered as part of this process.

Adoption

Intrinsic to the whole concept of adoption is the creation of a new family unit with new parent–child relationships. Children awaiting adoption are often encouraged to think about "new mummies and daddies". Prospective adopters anticipate that they will be able to form close, intimate relationships with their adopted children and experience the many dimensions of being a parent. Birth parents hope their children will be found a loving home where their new parents can give them opportunities and benefits which they themselves could not provide.

Adoption is not the same as having a birth child, however. Adoption means caring for and bringing up someone else's child. The additional elements of the adoptive parents' task have been clearly set out for many years, particularly by Brodzinsky *et al* (1998) (see Appendix 1), and a number of these tasks contain potential triggers to reconnect adopters with the pain and disappointment of their infertility. These extra dimensions also call for mature and robust parents, able to make positive use of their own life experiences in bringing up their children. It seems only sensible, therefore, to allow for opportunities during assessment and preparation when applicants can reflect carefully on the impact that infertility has had on them as individuals, on their primary relationship and on their wider relationships with family and friends.

Current situation

The changed adoption landscape of the 21st century also cannot be overlooked. The population of children requiring adoption has altered drastically in the last quarter of a century in particular. In 1968, the number of adoption orders granted in the UK was 27,500. In 2006, that figure had fallen to 4,764, including step-parent adoptions (Office for National Statistics, 2008, p. 141, table 6.16). Applicants unable to have birth children will, therefore, find far fewer children available than in the past.

"Straightforward", healthy, relinquished infants, those who formed the bulk of children placed for adoption in the 1960s and 1970s, are also much reduced in number. Increased access to contraception and termination, greater support for lone parents and changed values and sexual mores have all contributed to a situation where fewer expectant mothers regard adoption as their only choice.

Adoption boundaries have been pushed even further now that professionals no longer consider a child as being "unfit for adoption". The majority of children needing adoptive families today, therefore, are likely to be older, part of a sibling group or to have extra needs arising from disability or earlier harmful experiences.

Intercountry adoption has also become established in recent years and infertile applicants, often those who might be considered too old to adopt a very young child in this country, can now consider pursuing adoption from overseas.

Contact

Perhaps the greatest change of all is that it is now very common to find adopted children and young people who are still in touch with members of their birth family, including, in some instances, birth parents. In their large-scale study, *Supporting Adoption*, Lowe and Murch (1999) found that 77 per cent of adopted children were in touch with a member of their birth family, more than 50 per cent of them even after the granting of the adoption order. A far cry from the adoption scene of a generation ago, when adoption tended to close the door on the birth family.

This different adoption scene has, in turn, led to a recognition of the need for greater and longer lasting levels of post-placement and post-adoption support: for adopters, adopted children and also for birth families. Ongoing involvement with professional services, including social work, is therefore a real probability for today's adopters.

Exploring infertility

While the taboo subject of infertility is undoubtedly examined during adoption assessments, there is still some diffidence on the part of assessing workers to intrude unduly into this personal, intimate area of applicants' lives. Yet it is frequently a central motivating factor behind the adoption application and its relevance to the lifelong task ahead is undeniable. The journey from attempting to conceive your own child, ultimately via infertility investigation and treatment, to considering the adoption of someone else's two- and four-year-old children, who will have contact with birth grandparents, is considerable. It is essential that both applicant and assessor understand that journey, that there is confidence in prospective adopters' ability to embrace adoption as a positive choice and evidence that they have adequately integrated and can continue to cope with the complex emotions which infertility brings, possibly throughout life.

The purpose of this guide is to highlight some of the facets of this complex and emotive topic, to draw attention to areas which require exploration and to suggest ways in which to determine how applicants' infertility might impact on their adoption application. Whilst it is primarily intended to be useful to assessing social workers, it is hoped it might also be of interest to others such as fertility counsellors. Throughout the text, we have referred to "infertility" rather than "childlessness" and have used "subfertility" only as employed by the Human Fertilisation and Embryology Authority (HFEA) in its publications.

The topic of infertility is vast, and not every aspect can be tackled in a publication such as this. We offer, at best, some suggestions for useful ways of looking at it. In reality, each person's experience of it will differ and their responses will be highly individual. Not everyone who experiences infertility even wants to have children, whereas for others, a life without them just cannot be contemplated. In concentrating on those who pursue adoption, we do not intend any disrespect to those who, faced with infertility, choose, or are obliged to pursue, a life without parenthood, nor do we seek to devalue their lives. We have, therefore, limited ourselves to reflecting on parenthood today and considering the causes and consequences of infertility; issues stemming from assisted conception; understanding the emotional impact of infertility; the implications for adoption, including assessment, the processes of matching and placement; and finally, the lifelong issues. A brief appendix of assessment tools is also included (see Appendix 4).

Parenthood – attitudes and expectations

This chapter looks briefly at some aspects of parenthood in contemporary Britain: a large subject but an important one, because it provides the background against which infertility is experienced and adoption takes place. We briefly examine:

- attitudes to parenthood in contemporary Britain;

- hopes and expectations of parenthood;

- how these are realised, initially through pregnancy and childbirth and subsequently in bringing up children.

Here, we try to view parenthood largely from the perspective of people who hoped to be parents but have not succeeded in having children. They have had the same hopes and aspirations as those for whom parenthood is easily achieved. In looking at parenthood sequentially, it is important to bear in mind that that is not how it is experienced. Hopes and plans made at the beginning of life may become irrelevant and even be forgotten at times but they never entirely go away. Pregnancy and childbirth are only the first stage of life with a child but they are major life events, easily and often recalled. Conversely, if dreams for a life with children do not materialise and a much-desired pregnancy is never achieved, these can prove to be lifelong disappointments.

Before discussing these aspirations and disappointments with applicants for adoption, social workers need to be aware of their own views of children and the significance of family life. At a personal level, they may or may not share a would-be adopter's view of the desirability of giving birth, nurturing babies or of filling one's life with children. Cheerful remarks about 'missing all those sleepless nights and dirty nappies' when discussing the needs of children past infancy, may not be welcome to prospective adopters who have yearned to care for a baby. Conversely, social workers will encounter applicants for whom the process of giving birth is genuinely unimportant compared with the long-term joys and challenges of parenthood – a burden which the worker may find difficult to comprehend, particularly given the challenging nature of today's adoptive children.

Parenthood in contemporary Britain

Despite an ongoing trend towards smaller families, children are not only welcomed in Britain for the personal happiness and fulfilment they bring, they are also thought to be essential for the well-being of society itself and to represent its future. There is concern if birth rates fall below replacement level, lest this should lead to social atrophy and an inability to support an ageing population. At a national level, children are seen as a state responsibility. There is a consensus that adult lives and potential are shaped by childhood experiences and that the state has to have an important role in supporting all children and their parents. Hence, maternity and paternity leave around the time of birth, state benefits to support the child in the family and a massive public investment in child health and education are now seen as the essential foundations of a good society, with safety nets in place to protect the most vulnerable from cruelty and neglect.

Celebrating children

We are today a diverse society, incorporating many ethnic groups and a great variety of cultures, in all of which children are treasured as never before. Today's small families make the advent of a newcomer a cause for celebration. The birth of a child is eagerly anticipated and the joy and interest, rituals and present-giving with which a baby is received are heartfelt. Throughout childhood, each ethnic or religious group has its own way of showing its appreciation of its children and marking special days in a child's life. Our relative affluence has meant that today's babies and children can be indulged as never before. Many families can afford to give their children a healthy lifestyle, richer in opportunities than their forebears, although, by contrast, children are also among the most likely group in our society to experience poverty.

Childlessness

At a personal level, those who choose not to have children are not well understood by the majority. They may be viewed as selfishly clinging to an indulgent adult lifestyle. Any altruistic desire not to overpopulate the world gains little credit. For some people who crave parenthood and cannot achieve it, it can seem as if the world is against them and they are excluded from it:

> *At a practical level, even though parents complain bitterly about the child-unfriendliness of the British scene, childless couples especially will quickly tell you how the entire world is designed for families, from the ground up. The calendar revolves around school holidays. If you don't have children, but would like children, you notice the commercial world is designed to service families and singles, but not people like yourself.* (May, 2005, p. 71)

Plans and expectations

A stake in the future

Central to people's desire to procreate seems to be the sense that children give their parents a stake in the future. Rawlings and Looi (2007, pp. 24–5), looking at why some men desire to have children, list 'pride', 'immortality', and men's 'competitive nature': all of them linked to a desire for someone of one's own bloodline to fulfil one's own ambitions. They are not the only writers to reflect on the essential selfishness of people's hopes and dreams for the future. Black and Scull (2005), who have gathered the reflections of over 200 childless women, agree, and some of their respondents spelt it out (p. 39):

> *We are all a bit selfish, I think, actually having children to some extent it's about having something in your own image.*

> *I believe that children are what you leave behind, sort of thing, they're your legacy, in a way. That really, they are the only thing you leave behind, apart from memories that other people have of you, your children are what hopefully will be what carries on your genes throughout time.*

Children also carry the hopes of their wider family, as a Jewish respondent comments:

> *It's about . . . carrying on the line and family . . . family's really important . . . I grew up in a very close, Jewish family, very much family orientated, everything was around the family.*

For some people, this may translate into a particular desire for boy children to carry on the male line and the family name.

A parent in waiting

Many people have carried an image of themselves as a mother or father since early childhood, as one of the authors of *Beyond Childlessness* explains:

> *I (Rachel) can't recall a time when I didn't assume I'd have children. Playing at being mummy, keeping house, naming and caring for dolls, I understood from a very early age I was practising being a mum.* (Black and Scull, 2005, p. 24)

To not be able to have children goes against people's whole sense of who they are. A fertility counsellor likens it to weaving a rich tapestry which cannot be unpicked:

> *People grow up with the assumption that they will get pregnant. It is locked so deep into most female psyche to be a mother. It's like they weave a tapestry throughout their life and each experience, each part fills in more of it, more of the picture that it's going to be. Then when they are told or realise that this is not going to happen, they are left with all the work and the tapestry that cannot be undone.* (Black and Scull, 2005, p. 25)

Brebner *et al*, writing about infertile adopters of babies in the 1980s, agree about the size of this task:

> *Individuals who during their young years have seen their future selves not only as husbands and wives, but as parents, have to make a tremendous psychological adjustment to their infertility. They face not only the loss of self as the kind of person they would have become but the loss of the imaginary family and with it the kind of life they would have led. This adjustment may well be the most difficult that motherly or fatherly individuals will ever have to face.* (1985, p. 37)

This sense of being a parent-to-be will most probably be reinforced by family attitudes, especially when individuals are married or seen to be in settled partnerships. Many people, having brought up their own children, are eager to fulfil their own self-image as grandparents and feel impatience and frustration when grandchildren do not appear.

A biological urge

Although not everyone has a strong desire to have children, others talk of experiencing a strong "biological urge" to bear children. When thinking about when to have children and how large a family, most people are strongly influenced by their peers, by prevailing social and economic factors and by the

4

traditions of their own particular culture. Today's parents of first babies often recount how, all of a sudden, everyone in their social circle seems to feel it is the right time to move on to parenthood and the "biological urge", perhaps suppressed for years, suddenly becomes overwhelming. It is commonly assumed that this is felt most strongly, if not exclusively, by women, but Rawlings and Looi disagree, claiming that some men also have a biological clock which 'can tick pretty strongly':

> *On average, men underestimate how much they want children. They are trained in our society not to be child-focused. Some feel that children are an optional extra. But when they discover that they may miss out, it can be quite devastating.* (2007, p. 24)

It is a sad irony of modern life that social pressures to ignore the ticking clock until nearly midnight result in the need for children becoming urgent just as the likelihood of achieving them diminishes and this can catch people unawares:

> *It almost never occurs to you, you see, that you just might not be able to. That you might not be able to have your partner's child. That your parents might never get to enjoy spoiling their grandchildren. That you might never get to be a grandparent yourself.* (James, 2006, pp. 1–2)

Pregnancy and childbirth

A very special experience

> *It is something every woman should have a chance to experience, if she wants to. To feel a baby growing inside her. To give life to another human being.* (James, 2006, p. 2)

> *However much friends have told me that it's not always a good experience, I wanted that experience. It seems to me there's something very basic and primeval about being a woman and being pregnant and I wanted that experience.* (Black and Scull, 2005, p. 31)

Now that childbirth is safer than it has ever been and women are able to control their fertility so that they need not be pregnant year in, year out, the advantages of *not* experiencing pregnancy and childbirth are harder to perceive. Moreover, with the arrival of sophisticated techniques for treating infertility, it becomes harder by the year to accept that a pregnancy and subsequent birth are not

something that can be everyone's by right. Not everyone feels that "primeval" need but for the many who do, it is an experience to be treasured and to be painfully regretted if it does not happen.

Intimacy and intensity

It seems equally, if not more special, in some fundamental way, to be able to welcome one's newborn and share its first days and weeks in the world. As Winnicott points out:

> *The mother of a baby is tasting real things, and she would not miss the experience for the world.* (1964, p. 16)

Fathers too, even though they may not have anticipated it:

> *Do men behave the same [as women]? No, they don't gather in groups admiring tiny cardigans or discussing the benefits of nursing pads. Men usually don't talk to their friends about the dream to hold their own child. But . . . ask any first-time father as he is holding his newborn son 30 seconds after he is delivered if he misses his "freedom". The answer will always be 'no'.* (Rawlings and Looi, 2007, p. 24)

The intensity of these early hours and days is of course a biological necessity for the baby and the parents' bond with it. Conversely, foregoing that experience can leave a woman, especially, feeling that her body is redundant and its functions pointless:

> *There was this feeling, there's no point in having breasts, there's no point in having a uterus, there's no point in having periods, there's no point in sex, and I think I felt very alienated from my body . . . I just lost my body. There was no point to it.* (Black and Scull, 2005, p. 32)

The magical intimacy of life with a tiny baby is something that most people treasure in memory and women often speak of their pride and wonder at having been able to produce such an amazing little being. From first greetings and the noting of family likenesses, to what one of Black and Scull's respondents called 'that monkey thing, that sort of cuddling thing' (2005, p. 35); from breastfeeding to encouraging your baby's first smile and gurgle, these are special delights which more than compensate for the inevitable fatigue and the sense of failure and bewilderment when the baby's crying cannot be understood or assuaged. Not everyone who has had a baby looks back at the experience with undiminished pleasure and, for some, the bad memories definitely outweigh the good but that does not make them less enviable for those who desire the experience and have had to forego it. And it is the majority experience. Just as all the world quite suddenly seemed to want to be pregnant, now everyone is sharing baby conversations and taking parental leave from work. It is a lonely thing to be excluded from this new world, just at the point when everyone else seems to be entering it.

Bringing up a family

People who experience infertility will comfort themselves that, although they will have had to forego the experience of creating a baby and nurturing a newborn, that need not mean that children cannot play a significant role in their lives and vice versa. For some, the opportunity to be aunts and uncles, step-parents or godparents may be fulfilling enough, without the need to parent. Others will look to adoption as a way to build a family and take on a lifelong parental role.

Becoming a family

It is a cliché that bringing up children is "the most difficult job in the world". Many people feel they have not quite achieved full adulthood until they become parents themselves and take on its responsibilities. It is both a delight and a challenge to switch focus from the demands of work and adult pleasures to parenthood but for most people it marks a welcome shift to a new phase of life and underlines a couple's commitment to each other:

> *A child can also be seen from within the relationship as an expression of love. You love your partner enough to create something that is uniquely part of both of you.* (Rawlings and Looi, 2007, p. 25)

Part of seeing yourself as fully adult at last is to want to create your own family with its own culture and traditions, as these respondents of Black and Scull report (2005, p. 29):

> *What I'd wanted to do was to create a family, not just a husband and wife unit.*

> *It's the silly little things that I just thought would be rather wonderful to have – to nurture young people coming up and to get them to look back and think 'That's the way we did it in our family, that's what we had as our way of doing it'.*

A role for life

To become a parent is to take on a role for life that everyone hopes to perform well. There is no consensus as to exactly how that role should be played even within our own society. Neither is there any nationally agreed formula for success but most parents-to-be would share Rachel Black's dream of 'a child to love, to care for, to nurture and to teach' (Black and Scull, 2005, p. 35). They hope ultimately to be able to let their child move away confidently into adult life. Although the "giving" element is uppermost in people's minds as they assume responsibility for their small children, new parents are also clear that the relationship is reciprocal and that they themselves will reap rewards in the present and in the long-term future from the sense of belonging that they and their children will share.

In order to achieve their aims, parents employ a thousand strategies but most depend to a greater or lesser extent on:

- building a loving bond from babyhood;
- developing a parenting style of their own;
- shaping the child's world;
- gradually letting go.

In taking on these tasks, they will be "normal", in the way that some infertile couples so ardently desire:

> *I just want to be at home in the garden, have a little child, have a happy family and be "normal", as we're all led to believe it's "normal" to have a family.* (Black and Scull, 2005, p. 42)

They will also have to be heroic, in that the demands of parenthood are constant and the challenge to their endurance, wits and imagination endless. Moreover, family life will be played out against the background of public and private events which will bring their own joys and sorrows, triumphs and disappointments. Sometimes the social context which people inhabit will seem supportive: perhaps a comfortable home, with helpful neighbours and a good school and efficient health services to hand. At other times, or for other people, the reverse may be true and life becomes a struggle and a disappointment.

Later in life, some parents will have frequent contact with their adult children and the pleasure of grandchildren, whilst others will be less fortunate. The majority will continue to feel some degree of responsibility towards their children in adulthood, even whilst they become in turn their children's responsibility towards old age.

ISSUES AND TASKS FOR SOCIAL WORKERS

- Be aware of your own views on and experiences of parenthood and how these may influence you as an assessing social worker.

- Be aware of the emphasis on children and parenthood which pervades most societies and cultures, and of societal views of "normal" families.

- Seek to identify the extent to which each individual's personal desire for children has been influenced by this atmosphere and by the attitudes and expectations of those close to them.

- Recognise that there may be subtle differences between wanting to be a parent and wanting to be like everyone else.

- In discussion with applicants, distinguish between the urge to experience pregnancy and birth and the nurture of a newborn baby and the desire to bring up a family, or help a child who has difficulties that are likely to prove long-lasting.

KEY MESSAGES

- Parenting is viewed positively in our society and is supported by it.

- How individual families express their delight in their children depends on their own ethnic and religious culture and family traditions.

- Pregnancy, childbirth and caring for a young baby are viewed by the majority as experiences to be highly prized.

- Bringing up children and, later in life, having a close relationship with adult children and grandchildren, is the experience of the majority in our society and has therefore come to be regarded as the norm.

2 Infertility – causes and implications

Although the impact of infertility is considered more fully in Chapter 4 and assessment issues in Chapter 6, this chapter will begin to highlight some of the issues which will confront prospective adopters who have received a diagnosis of infertility.

Infertility has many causes. While common, predominant feelings are likely to be present to some degree in all situations where people want to have a child and discover that they are infertile, it is important for assessing social workers to comprehend each individual's personal experience of infertility, the specific attendant emotions experienced at different points, and the implications for a subsequent adoption.

Investigation

Most people, hoping to start a family and finding it difficult, will usually choose to consult their GP and a referral to the local infertility clinic is likely. Choices have to be made at this point, therefore, even with emotions running high, since some couples will choose not to pursue investigations at all. While this is a very personal decision, the reasoning behind it needs to be clarified in an adoption assessment.

Social workers need to know whether the decision by applicants not to investigate their infertility is an indication of temperament, personal philosophy, or religious faith. Has the individual considered that the "problem" may be relatively easily resolved with help? Might there be a likelihood of later regret when treatment options are no longer available, for example, due to age? Is this a joint decision, or does only one partner have a strong desire to be a parent?

One experienced social worker told the authors that such a decision warranted a particularly careful exploration in case it pointed to a vulnerability in the relationship:

> *Is the marriage consummated? How, as a couple, are they able to deal with health issues or feelings? Is it that the relationship is not robust enough to survive a finding that it's one of the couple's problem? I really need to know.*
> (Personal communication)

Treatment

Some couples will be asked to consider assisted conception and the various techniques are discussed in Chapter 3. Not everyone wishes to pursue this route, however, and again an understanding of the reasoning behind this decision is essential. Many people have the perception that waiting lists are long and treatment success rates low and choose not to expose themselves to invasive and, at times, uncomfortable and upsetting procedures. Age and finances may also come into the equation, since not everyone will be able to pay for private in-vitro fertilisation (IVF) attempts. Others may not wish to conceive a child who is genetically unrelated to one of the partners. If such decisions were taken, how were they reached and what is their relevance for adoption?

It is not unusual for adoption workers to be meeting with couples who have exhausted every available treatment option and who have spent years of their lives, and sometimes large sums of money, trying to conceive. Attempts may even have gone on unrealistically and against all odds. What interpretation can an assessor legitimately put on such circumstances? Have the applicants found coping strategies which have enabled them to move on? Why do they consider it appropriate to be making an application for adoption now? Can this couple realistically contemplate the adoption of a child who is past babyhood and who has additional needs?

Many couples will take a middle road, pursuing treatment for a while, until it no longer seems the best option, either because it is unlikely to succeed, or because the process is becoming excessively protracted or financially too demanding. Sometimes considerable time has passed since treatment ended and applicants themselves will readily talk about how and why their needs and attitudes have changed since they embarked on treatment.

Causes of infertility

There are many causes of infertility. Difficulties can lie with either a male or female partner; both may have a problem; or infertility may be unexplained.

Regardless of the cause, the end result is the same, although the implications may vary depending on the reason for the failure to conceive. A number of common themes emerge, however, which should not be ignored. Below, we look at some of the main reasons for male and female infertility and some of the common emotional reactions.

Male infertility

There is a wide range of conditions which may render a man infertile. Among the most common are:

- low sperm count;
- no viable sperm;
- poor sperm motility.

In all of these situations, it is probable that the individual will have enjoyed normal sexual relations with no indication that anything might be amiss. Occasionally, such as when there have been earlier treatments for some cancers, a man will know from the outset of a heterosexual relationship that he is incapable of fathering a child. He may even have been given the opportunity to store some of his sperm prior to cancer treatment.

A diagnosis of infertility in a man can often strike at the individual's fundamental sense of self. The siring of children, getting a partner pregnant, are historically linked with perceptions of virility and strength, and a man who cannot do that may well feel much less of a man or that his sexual prowess or performance is in doubt. In some cultures, infertility in men may be inadmissible, as a British Asian wife explains to Black and Scull:

> *My husband has a problem, not me. If I'd got a problem, I'd be out of his life. Asian people, especially gents, they don't understand, they don't accept that there should be a fault in them, all the time they think the fault is with the woman . . . [The doctor] said, 'He has the problem, not you'. My husband never accepted it, he said, 'No, I'm OK'.* (2005, p. 129)

Even when a diagnosis of infertility is accepted, men often seem uncomfortable discussing it and can be prey to very basic and irrational fears which they sometimes cannot share, even with a partner. Social pressure may even take a direct and ribald form, feeding these fears and underlining feelings of sexual inadequacy. Bentley writes:

> *Being infertile made me question just how much of a man I really was. It is not something you can easily discuss with friends. The way men talk about infertility – terms such as "jaffa" (as in seedless oranges) and "starting pistol" (firing blanks) – makes it a really sensitive subject to bring up . . . Rather than talk about it I found myself internalising the guilt and the shame and anger.* (2007, p. 3)

It should be noted, however, that there may be some instances where infertility is as a result of the male partner's impotence, an inability to achieve or maintain an erection or to reach ejaculation. While medical assistance may be of help in some cases, there will be other situations where treatment is of little benefit. A satisfying and enjoyable sexual relationship can be a central strength in a partnership and if frustrations, disappointment and even anger feature, there can be direct implications for adoption.

Female infertility

Historically, women appear to have carried most of the burden surrounding infertility and in some cultures can still be divorced or returned to their families if they are found to be "barren" and unable to produce a male heir. The reasons for female infertility are many and varied but those most frequently encountered include:

- complex menstrual history/failure to ovulate/early menopause;
- blocked fallopian tubes;
- endometriosis;
- inability to carry a foetus to term;
- specific conditions, e.g. Turner's Syndrome;
- as a consequence of treatment for a medical condition, e.g. cancer of the womb or ovaries.

As with their male partners, many women will be unaware of specific problems although, in some instances, some will have experienced irregular or abnormal menstruation. There will have been no difficulties in a sexual relationship with a partner and the first sign that all is not well will be the absence of pregnancy.

Sometimes, however, a woman may not be able to permit full sexual intercourse. Feelings of inadequacy and shame might be present for a woman in such circumstances, while a man could feel excluded, frustrated and disappointed. If there are such central elements of dissatisfaction in any relationship, then it can be rendered vulnerable, particularly if the dynamic is to be altered by the placement of a child.

Irregularities in the menstrual cycle may have prepared a woman for fertility problems and for some individuals, it will be important that they have sought full medical advice about their situation. Sometimes medication may, relatively easily, regulate a woman's periods or stimulate ovulation and many people would gladly undertake drug treatment to achieve a greater likelihood of becoming pregnant.

For women, however, the probability of invasive investigations or even surgical interventions is much higher than for men. Blood tests can determine if a woman is ovulating but, in other situations, it may be necessary to consider a wide range of other procedures including ultra-sound scanning, x-rays or laparoscopy. In the latter procedure, dye is injected via the cervix and a tube is inserted with a tiny camera attached, to check for blockages in the fallopian tubes.

While surgery to deal with blockages caused by, for example, scar tissue or fibroids may still be offered, in-vitro fertilisation and intra-cytoplasmic sperm injection techniques (see Chapter 3) are now much more advanced and available, so that an operation may not be indicated.

For a woman to confront the fact that her reproductive system is "faulty" or that conception will only be possible with technological assistance, can produce emotions of failure and inadequacy. One of life's natural, fundamental functions is not possible for her and her sense of completeness as a woman can be overwhelmingly assaulted. A woman still struggling with such powerful feelings may well not be completely emotionally freed-up to invest in the adoption of another woman's child or to deal with the lifelong reminders of her pain which an adopted child might trigger.

Some medical conditions or previous illnesses or surgery will mean that infertility has been a known factor from the outset. For some women, this can again result in feelings that they are deficient or flawed and while the adjustment to such a circumstance might, arguably, be more easily accomplished since it has always been known, a degree of resolution still has to be achieved, at least to the point when there is no undue vulnerability.

Miscarriage

A proportion of women will be able to conceive but pregnancies will ultimately result in miscarriage. In such cases of secondary infertility, medical supervision or assistance may achieve a live birth. For those women where this does not happen, however, the physical and emotional drain of failed pregnancy, sometimes at a relatively late stage, cannot be overlooked. Conception brings hope and a miscarriage can be experienced not only as the end of that hope but as an actual bereavement, the loss of an identifiable life. The Miscarriage Association (see Useful Organisations) stresses that this is 'a very unhappy, frightening and lonely experience'.

Repeated pregnancies and miscarriages intensify that experience and the constant hope, the recurring disappointment and frustration over what so nearly might have been are significant emotional experiences which need to be understood in the context of an adoption application.

Unexplained infertility

In a number of cases, no clear cause for infertility can be established. No abnormalities are detected in either partner, the sexual relationship is problem-free but no pregnancy results. Individuals will often have been subject to numerous tests over a period of time and have had countless disappointments without, arguably, the relief of knowing that there is a problem which explains matters.

Would-be adopters in this position have described the pain of living in almost constant hope, unable to lay the issue of their infertility to rest and perpetually wrestling with the frustration of simply not knowing why there is no baby when there are no obvious contra-indications to a pregnancy. Black and Scull comment that 'while there is still hope of fulfilling the dream of having a child, it can be hard to avoid putting other aspects of your life on hold' (2005, p. 56).

As in all cases of infertility, individuals can question whether they should stay together or allow their partner to find another, fertile mate. Is there merely some undetected incompatibility and might children be possible with another partner? Understanding of the process of accommodation of unexplained fertility within the relationship, not least in decisions around contraception, is clearly necessary before embarking on adoption.

Becoming infertile

Some people will previously have been fertile and may even have had children prior to their adoption application. Relatively common situations include:

- sterilisation in a previous relationship;
- illness, accident or a health condition;
- infertility as a result of infection.

An added complication in such cases results when one or even both partners no longer have the care of previous children. In some instances, children may live with the other parent or even have been surrendered to adoption or the care of relatives. The contrast between the previous situation and the applicants' current infertile state is stark.

If the current infertility is due to past behaviours, for example, a sexually transmitted disease, it is probable that the individual will feel not only regret but a significant amount of guilt. Assimilating and adjusting to this set of circumstances is a significant task for many individuals and partnerships.

Involuntary childlessness

There are many circumstances in which people choose not to have children, most of which are not the concern of this book. There are, however, some people who have to leave their fertility untested, sometimes to their deep regret, and may turn to adoption as a consequence. In particular, these might include those for whom there might be a genetic risk to any child conceived, gay men, lesbians and single people.

Genetic risk

Some prospective parents can find themselves in a position where a pregnancy is possible but carries the risk that the child may be significantly affected by a genetic condition. Couples may have already experienced the trauma of elective terminations and have had counselling which has led to the decision not to risk further pregnancies. To voluntarily relinquish the chance of parenthood may, in some circumstances, be a painful but unavoidable decision, whilst for others, the issues may be less clear-cut.

Gay or lesbian applicants

Many gay or lesbian applicants for adoption may well be fertile but will obviously not have been able to produce a child with a same-sex partner. Others may know of their infertility or have not pursued testing. Regardless of individual circumstances, confronting feelings about childlessness can be inextricably linked with accepting one's sexual orientation. This may also prove to be an issue for some assessors, who may feel diffident about exploring such a private matter, but such a central component of a would-be adopter's life cannot simply be ignored (see Mallon and Betts, 2005, p. 37).

Others may consider that being gay or lesbian automatically means that there will be no children and so, reflecting on a given state of childlessness, or possibly infertility, is not required. No matter how secure an individual is in his or her sexuality, however, there can still be regrets that this has precluded offspring created with a life partner. These regrets or losses need to be sufficiently integrated, just as for heterosexual applicants, to allow confident decision-making on adoption.

Gay and lesbian applicants who are fertile do have choices other than adoption, however. They, and ultimately their workers, need to be aware of these possible options, since an assessor will be more assured in making a recommendation if there is understanding on both sides of how the decision to seek adoption was reached. Choices include:

- for both men and women, seeking a heterosexual, sexual relationship or encounter;
- for women, self-fertilisation using donated sperm;
- for men, donating sperm and contracting to be involved in the upbringing of the resultant child;
- for women, fertility treatment such as IVF;
- for both men and women, entering into a surrogacy arrangement.

Some of these options may very readily and understandably be ruled out by gay and lesbian applicants but others may warrant careful thought.

Single applicants

Prospective adopters with no partner may also have some of the choices outlined for gay and lesbian applicants above. For single applicants, however, there may, in addition to disappointment that there are to be no children, be feelings of inadequacy given their single status. Societal pressures, as described earlier, impinge on single individuals as well as couples, and while some people make a positive choice not to enter into a partnership, others will not be immune to the prevalent expectation that people will eventually pair off and produce children. Single individuals who then consider adoption can harbour anxieties that they will be seen as "less eligible" than couples (see Owen, 1999, p. 53).

Cultural issues

Understanding the pressures to which infertile applicants have been subject prior to making an adoption application is vitally important. These pressures and the way in which they have been experienced will vary in each case and general assumptions must not be made about any specific culture or community.

Nevertheless, as noted in Chapter 1, there may be some ethnic communities where the emphasis on continuing a family name or producing a male heir is considerable. The disappointment evident within the family circle when no child appears may be palpable and an additional, ever-present burden for a couple or individual to carry, together with attendant and peculiarly intense feelings of shame and failure.

Attitudes to adoption

Perceptions and experience of adoption vary between individuals and between cultures. For some people, there could be real obstacles, for example, to the placement of a child whose antecedents are not known, or who originated from a different religious, albeit not a different ethnic, grouping. Such "discrimination" on the part of families may cause alarm or disquiet in assessing social workers and it will be important for agencies to understand such issues within the cultural context and to be clear about the stance to be taken.

Producing a child prior to marriage, or failing to care adequately for a child to the point when alternative parents have to be found, may result in culturally prescribed strong feelings about the "immoral" or deficient parent. These emotions may be particularly strong in some cultures and can also attach to the child, rendering adoption a process fraught with risks for all concerned. Obtaining information on how applicants' culture and faith might have influenced their journey to adoption, and might continue to impinge over the years, will clearly, therefore, be essential. This is especially the case if applicants belong to a minority ethnic grouping about whom the assessor may know little.

Applicants' attitudes to the process of adoption will also vary greatly according to their pre-existing views on social workers and their professional activities. Just as social workers might bring to the process preconceived notions about people seeking to adopt after infertility, so applicants may approach the enterprise with some negative ideas about social workers, e.g. that they are too young, too intrusive, too judgmental, etc. Applicants may expect the adoption process to be gruelling rather than constructive.

Adopting relatives from overseas

It is not uncommon to encounter situations where infertile applicants hope to adopt the child of a relative living overseas, perhaps in less stable or less well-developed areas of the world. The issues which arise in the assessment of related adoptive applicants have been well recognised and some of these will have especial relevance for infertile couples.

In Chapter 8, we discuss some of the lifelong factors for all infertile adopters, not least the task of establishing themselves as the parents of a child not born to them. The reminders of a child's parentage, which may be present at family gatherings or celebrations, the sense of being beholden to a known fertile donor and the fear of dealing, on an ongoing basis, with the "truth" of family relationships, are all matters which need to be acknowledged and carefully considered in relation to that core task.

ISSUES AND TASKS FOR SOCIAL WORKERS

- Be aware of the impact of infertility on individuals and relationships, whilst also being aware that all individuals will experience this in different ways.

- Be sensitive to the profound, gender-specific feelings which applicants may have experienced.

- Ensure that all routes to parenthood have been identified and considered to obviate later regrets about missed opportunities.

- Seek evidence on how powerful feelings have been processed and integrated, while respecting the applicants' need for dignity and privacy.

- Recognise that an application for adoption inevitably means discussing intimate areas of people's relationships, which requires tact and delicacy.

- For applicants who might still conceive, the worker needs to explore the issue of contraception.

KEY MESSAGES

- There are many reasons why individuals and couples cannot have children.

- The attendant feelings may vary, dependent on the cause, individual circumstances, temperament and even the gender of the infertile applicant.

- Primarily, however, emotions centre on loss, regret and failure.

- These emotions will need to be accommodated, at least to a degree, if applicants are to enter into adoption in the best position from which to form a bond with an adopted child.

- A good working relationship is needed between social worker and applicants if the delicate issues surrounding infertility are to be helpfully explored during an assessment.

3 Infertility investigation and treatment

This chapter and Chapter 4 look in more detail at what an infertile applicant for adoption may have experienced (and may still be experiencing) in the period leading up to their approach to their adoption agency. Here, we look in more detail at the process of infertility investigation and, specifically, treatment.

Most infertile applicants for adoption will already have spent a considerable period of time exploring their infertility and possible treatment options before they contact the adoption agency. They will have come from a very different "medical" world where the focus has been almost entirely on solving the problem and achieving a pregnancy. The emphasis of the adoption assessment and preparation process is very different and it is important that assessors have some understanding of what applicants might have experienced before beginning the journey to adoption. Each of the pathways to parenthood described below carries its own stresses and dilemmas, some of them painful and traumatic for the individual involved. It is important that these are discussed during an assessment as they can shed valuable light on how applicants have arrived at difficult decisions and how couples have helped each other through challenging times. The strength and determination required to persevere through infertility treatment should be recognised by assessing social workers.

Initial investigation

Individuals experiencing difficulty conceiving will probably first seek advice from their general practitioner. The Human Fertilisation and Embryology Authority (HFEA) suggests that couples should speak to their GP if they have been trying to conceive for 18 months to two years without success. If aged over 35, it is suggested that advice should be sought after a period of approximately six months. Fertility tests can take some time and age may affect the treatments available.

At the surgery, applicants can expect a physical examination and, for women, the probability of a cervical smear test, urine tests and blood tests to check ovulation. Men will also be given a urine test and will be asked to produce a sperm sample to test for any abnormalities. In most instances, if no obvious matters come to light, GPs will refer patients for further investigation, particularly if the couple are in their 30s, have been trying for a baby for over 18 months or are younger but have been trying for a baby for three years or more.

At the clinic

At the local hospital or fertility clinic, further tests may include blood tests to find out if the woman is ovulating; an ultrasound scan to look at the womb and ovaries; an x-ray to check fallopian tubes; follicle tracking – a series of ultrasound scans following the development of a follicle to see if an egg is developing; laparoscopy – an operation in which a dye is injected through the cervix and a camera inserted to check for tubal blockages; hysteroscopy – where a telescope with a camera attached is used to view the uterus to check for conditions such as fibroids or polyps. Sometimes, a vaginal ultrasound probe is used, again to check fallopian tubes for blockages. Very occasionally, a tissue sample may be taken from the lining of the womb for analysis. Men will again be asked to produce a sperm sample for semen analysis, a sperm antibody test may be carried out to check for protein molecules which may prevent sperm from fertilising an egg and there may be a sperm invasion test, to see if sperm are swimming through the cervical mucous and are still active. Not all of these tests, particularly for women, will be carried out simultaneously and so the period of investigation itself can take some time, particularly since results will not always be immediately available.

Treatment options: drugs and surgery

Drugs are not quite so important in the treatment of male infertility but occasionally may be prescribed. These could include antibiotics to treat infection or inflammation; vitamins to improve sperm movement (although there appears to be no convincing evidence for this treatment); drugs which close the neck of the bladder when sperm are being ejaculated to the bladder instead of to the penis; or gonadotrophin injections or pump administration for certain rare conditions in which no sperm is produced.

For women, particularly for those who are not ovulating or ovulating infrequently, fertility drugs, which trigger egg production in much the same way as the body's own hormones, may help. While such drug therapy may, of itself, result in pregnancy, it is much more likely that it will be used alongside other techniques. Most of these drugs can be grouped together under the heading ovulation-inducing drugs although, in some instances, it may be appropriate to use cycle-suppressing drugs or, at a later stage, drugs which maintain pregnancy, particularly in treatments where embryos are implanted in the womb. Given the advances in infertility treatment, it is not as common now to offer surgery even in situations where there are blocked tubes. Nevertheless, this may still be an option in some situations when keyhole surgery is most frequently used. In some situations, partners may have been sterilised and may seek a reversal. It is possible for a woman's fallopian tubes to be rejoined at the ends and success rates are higher if the sterilisation is relatively recent and the ends of the tubes were clipped rather than tied.

Male vasectomies can be reversed in some circumstances but if not, it is also possible to undergo a small operation known as surgical sperm retrieval where sperm is removed from the epididymis (where the sperm is actually made) or from the testicles and could then be used in subsequent assisted conception attempts.

Assisted conceptions

Intrauterine insemination (IUI)

IUI involves inserting sperm into the womb to coincide with ovulation. At present, this treatment is often used where there is unexplained infertility or ovulation problems have been identified. Clinics may recommend this procedure if the male partner's sperm count is low or has poor motility, or as a less invasive alternative to surgical intervention. It may also be recommended if a man is impotent or experiences premature ejaculation. In some instances, it may also have been identified that sperm is not surviving the journey through the cervical mucous which can sometimes be too thick to allow the sperm to pass through or because there may be antibodies present which attack the sperm. The procedure involves blood tests for the female to determine when she is ovulating, although sometimes it may be recommended that fertility drugs are also used to stimulate ovulation. These are often self-administered as an injection (requiring some discipline from the woman) or a nasal spray. Eggs are tracked by vaginal ultrasound scans as soon as they develop and as soon as an egg is mature, a hormone injection is administered to stimulate the egg's release. Sperm is inserted approximately 36 hours later using a speculum which will keep the vaginal walls apart. A small catheter is then inserted and sperm, previously provided by the male partner and treated, are then inserted via the catheter. The whole process takes only a few minutes and it is unlikely that the female partner will experience anything more than some discomfort.

It should be noted that some couples choose to attempt home insemination using a home insemination kit. Couples may also, at this point, have to give consideration to using donor sperm, particularly if specific problems are identified in the sperm produced by the male partner. This is a highly significant decision for many couples and some choose not to pursue this route since it will mean that one partner will not be the child's biological parent.

In-vitro fertilisation (IVF)

This is one of the best known and established fertility treatments, often described as "test-tube babies". IVF literally means "fertilisation in glass", with eggs being removed from the ovaries and fertilised with sperm in a laboratory dish before being placed in the woman's womb. It may well be recommended by the fertility clinic if the female partner is older, the couple have been diagnosed with unexplained infertility, the female has blockages in the fallopian tubes or other techniques, such as ovulation induction (IUI), have been unsuccessful. Techniques differ from clinic to clinic but many women's experience of IVF includes initial treatment to boost the egg supply. This involves drugs to block the hormones which are usually produced by the pituitary gland during a woman's monthly cycle. This allows better control over when eggs are produced. The woman then has further drug therapy to make the ovaries produce more than one egg. Vaginal ultrasound scans are again carried out to monitor the developing eggs. Clinics will also often do blood tests to chart the rising levels of oestrogen produced by the egg. As soon as the test shows that the time is right, the female receives another injection of a different hormone to help the eggs mature. Timing is crucial in this process since this injection must be administered 34–38 hours before the eggs are collected.

The next step involves collecting eggs by ultrasound guidance or, occasionally, by laparoscopy. Ultrasound guidance may involve a general anaesthetic and the use of vaginal ultrasound to produce pictures on a screen, which then allows the doctor to insert a thin needle through the vagina into each ovary. The needle is then guided into each egg sac in turn, sucking the egg into it. If a laparoscopy is conducted, this is also done under a general anaesthetic. A small telescope is inserted through a small cut in the stomach followed by a fine needle to remove the eggs. It is rare, nowadays, for this procedure to be used to collect eggs.

Around the time the partner's eggs are collected, the man produces a fresh sample of sperm. This will be stored for a short time before the sperm are washed and spun at a high speed so that the healthiest and the most active can be selected. If donor sperm is being used, the sample is taken from the freezer and prepared the same way.

The eggs are mixed with the partner's sperm and left in a laboratory dish for 18–20 hours before they are checked to see if they fertilise. Any that have not or any that have fertilised abnormally are discarded. The remaining embryos are then left for another 24–28 hours before being checked again.

Two days after the eggs have been collected, the woman is given progesterone via pessaries, injection or gel to help prepare the lining of the womb. Two to five days after fertilisation, one or two healthy embryos are usually chosen and put back into the womb through the cervix via a catheter. The decision about how many embryos are transferred is important because it affects not only the chances of conception but also the chance of having a multiple birth. Remaining embryos may be frozen for future IVF attempts if they are suitable. In some cases, embryos may not be implanted until they have developed for five to six days after fertilisation and may then be transferred at what is known as the blastocyst stage. In some instances, allowing the embryos to develop for longer can increase the chances of successful pregnancy.

Clearly, couples need to be guided by the staff at fertility clinics since not all treatments will be suitable in every case and each situation must be examined carefully to determine what, if any, problems are identified.

Intra-cytoplasmic sperm injections (ICSI)

This process involves injecting a single sperm into the cytoplasm or centre of an egg. This is generally seen as one of the most significant advances in infertility treatment since IVF. It was introduced in the 1990s and was hailed as a revolutionary development in treatment for male infertility.

It may be considered if a man's sperm count is very low, the sperm cannot move properly or are abnormally shaped or there are high levels of anti-sperm antibodies in a man's semen. It may be suggested if a couple have tried previous IVF treatment but few or no eggs have been fertilised. It may also be considered in situations where the female partner has responded poorly to ovarian stimulation, producing few eggs of which few have been able to be fertilised. It might also be considered if sperm has already been retrieved directly from the epididymis or the testicles.

Men will be asked to produce a fresh sperm sample on the same day as their partner's eggs are collected. The woman will take fertility drugs to stimulate the ovaries to produce more eggs which are collected on a certain day, as in the process for IVF. These are then fertilised with the partner's sperm and replaced in the womb in exactly the same way as for conventional IVF. Any suitable embryos not used at this stage can be frozen for future use.

Gamete intra-fallopian transfer (GIFT)

This is one of the earliest fertility treatments and is still being used today. It begins with gametes (eggs and sperm) being collected in exactly the same way as for IVF. The healthiest are chosen, mixed together and placed in one of the fallopian tubes. Fertilisation takes place inside the body just as it would have done had there not been medical intervention. It is used in situations of unexplained infertility when fallopian tubes are not blocked and appear undamaged. It may also be considered if a man has a low sperm count or sperm with low motility. Sometimes, IVF may be tried first to make sure a man's sperm can fertilise the female's egg. If successful, GIFT may be used in the next treatment cycle instead of repeating IVF.

Men are asked to provide a sperm sample on the same day as the eggs are collected. If donor sperm are being used, they are carefully stored before being mixed with the collected eggs. Before proceeding with this treatment, women may be given a uterine-dye test and a laparoscopy to check that the fallopian tubes are healthy and clear. Up to the point of egg collection, GIFT is exactly the same procedure as for IVF.

Under anaesthetic, a laparoscope will be inserted through a small cut in the abdomen to view the womb and the fallopian tube. The healthiest one or two eggs are then mixed with the prepared sperm in a catheter which is inserted to deposit the eggs at the end of one or both fallopian tubes nearest the womb. The woman needs a short rest before going home and will be given some progesterone via injections, pessaries, or gel, again to build up the lining of the womb.

Donors

It is not the intention to explore this topic in any depth, since other organisations such as the HFEA provide comprehensive and accessible literature on this topic. Infertile couples embarking on treatment, however, will find that they may have to consider using donated sperm or eggs at some point in the procedure, dependent on the circumstances contributing to their infertility. For some couples, the choice is clear since they would not wish one parent to be the biological parent while the other is not, as stated earlier. For others, there will be anxieties about having to explain this in the future to any resulting child. These are very significant, emotive issues which applicants may have tussled with along the way to making an application for adoption.

Frozen embryos

Another difficult area for couples is the storage and freezing of embryos for possible future attempts at, for example, IVF. Questions about how long to store embryos and what to do with them if further attempts are not needed or not embarked upon, exercise couples considerably and there is a public debate about the ethics and morality of this whole procedure. Conscious of this, many couples feel under great pressure and find these decisions difficult, if not impossible, to make.

Surrogacy

Surrogacy is a very complicated legal area and couples should only consider embarking on it after they have taken clear, independent legal advice. Some couples may consider surrogacy if the woman has a medical condition which makes it impossible or dangerous for her to become pregnant and give birth. It may also be an option which couples explore following unsuccessful IVF treatment. Few couples choose this route at present, although some do consider it, perhaps involving a member of the wider family.

Basically, surrogacy is when another woman carries and gives birth to a baby for someone else. There are two ways of having a baby with a surrogate. Sperm from the male partner can be mixed with the surrogate's eggs, usually by artificial insemination or

IUI – this is called full surrogacy. It may also be possible to use the woman's eggs and the man's sperm or donated eggs inseminated with the partner's sperm. This involves IVF, which must take place in a licensed clinic, and is called partial surrogacy.

Following the birth of a child, the legal mother of the birth child is the surrogate and her name will appear on the birth certificate. If the surrogate is married, her husband will usually be the legal father of the child and his name will appear on the birth certificate. In Scotland, however, it is possible for the male partner's name to be placed on the birth certificate alongside that of the surrogate and this will give him parental rights and responsibilities. In due course, a commissioning couple needs to seek a parental order under s.30 of the Human Fertilisation and Embryology Act 1990 or an adoption order. A fertility clinic involved in any surrogacy arrangement must be assured that an adoption agency is involved in the process before treatment will be provided.

Counselling

Some couples may be referred to support groups for individuals experiencing fertility problems and there is also a significant number of internet support sites run by people who have had similar experiences. Counselling and support organisations are also listed at the end of this guide.

All fertility clinics licensed by the HFEA must offer implications counselling before applicants consent to treatment. This involves a counsellor talking to the couple about the treatment they may have, so that they understand exactly what is involved and how it might affect them and those close to them. This can be particularly important if couples are considering treatment with donated eggs, sperm, embryos or surrogacy, which all involve complicated issues.

If couples need emotional support before, during, or after fertility treatment, support counselling is available at many clinics. Couples can be given written information and, if they need additional support, can be put in touch with other local services. Infertility can throw up all sorts of issues. For some individuals, it can trigger painful memories from the past or the treatment that they are undertaking may result in feelings of depression or increased anxiety. Therapeutic counselling assists individuals to work through some of these issues and can help to deal with the impact that infertility may be having on the individual's life and relationships.

It is helpful for a subsequent assessing social worker to know what counselling was offered to applicants and how this was utilised. Bingley Miller, in the British Infertility Counselling Association's guide, *Adoption: Issues for infertility counsellors* (2005, p. 3) stresses the importance of exploring each individual's perception of adoption. Exploring fantasies and feelings is also seen as useful and assessors may find that applicants have done significant early ground-work in counselling sessions prior to making an application.

Finance

It is worth recognising that not all infertility treatment may be available on the NHS, or treatment may be limited to one or two attempts. At HFEA-licensed clinics, it may be possible for couples to pay for their treatment or further attempts at a particular process but costs are considerable and the cost of a counsellor may also have to be met from the individuals' own funds. Not every couple is in a position to meet such expenses and, for many couples, there may be no clinic within easy travelling distance, necessitating extra expense and upheaval in order to attend for consultations and treatment.

ISSUES AND TASKS FOR SOCIAL WORKERS

- **Gain some understanding of how these applicants reached their decision to proceed or not at each stage of the process, including the use made of counselling.**

- **Be aware of the "climate of hope" in which the applicants will have existed during treatment.**

- **Recognise the determination and perseverance that is needed to undergo infertility treatments of this kind.**

- **Reflect with applicants on how they coped and supported each other during a prolonged period of uncertainty.**

- **Be sensitive to the fact that many aspects of the process may have been experienced as mechanical, distasteful and even risky. Both partners may feel traumatised by these processes.**

- **Do not lose sight of the fact that a long and perhaps difficult period has ended for these applicants.**

KEY MESSAGES

- **The causes of infertility are many and varied and may indicate different treatment options.**

- **Infertility investigation and treatment can feel invasive, clinical and even harrowing for both partners.**

- **Treatment can take a huge physical and emotional toll on applicants.**

- **The world of infertility clinics is medically orientated and can feel disempowering.**

 # The impact of infertility

This chapter will begin a closer examination of the impact of infertility on individuals, couples and their families, and how they cope with it. It underlines the possible implications for adoption which, in turn, will be examined specifically in Chapter 6.

Bereavement or journey?

For many people who find themselves unable to have children, the experience of infertility is deeply traumatic and may represent the single most devastating blow they have suffered in their lives so far. It has been usual to regard this experience as a kind of bereavement in that it involves having to give up hopes of parenthood, a state prized by many people (see Chapter 1). Like all bereavements, this one can then be thought of as having a number of stages, likely to be experienced to a greater or lesser extent:

- loss;
- grief;
- resolution;
- moving on.

This perspective, however, has its limitations and will not apply equally to everyone. Loss of the expectation of parenthood is only part of the picture, as a diary of one couple's experience of infertility treatment, which could stand for many, demonstrates (see Appendix 3). Three recurrent themes run through Susan's account:

- the endurance of physical pain and discomfort;
- the effort and discipline needed to stay the course and give each cycle of treatment its best chance of success;
- the seesaw of emotion as hopes of success are repeatedly dashed.

These themes suggest more similarity to an expedition undertaken in extremely challenging circumstances and which ends in disappointment, rather than to a bereavement. It is, indeed, quite usual to find the endeavour to overcome infertility described as a journey. Both concepts can be useful in making sense of people's stories but some infertile people will not feel that either concept describes their own experience. What seems certain is that it is a deeply individual experience to which people respond differently, according to:

- the nature of their infertility;
- the course of any treatment;
- their circumstances;
- their personality and previous experience of trauma;
- the support they receive from those closest to them.

A careful and attentive listener to applicants telling their own story in their own words is best placed to grasp its complexities and appreciate the sheer variety of events and emotions that it has encompassed.

Unwelcome news

The discovery of their infertility and the start of the journey (if that is how it is seen), occurs at different times in an individual's life and in different circumstances. Perhaps the most common experience is of a gradual, disheartening realisation of a problem when no pregnancy occurs, followed by confusion, alternating hope, sadness and even despair as investigations and treatment proceed. This is movingly illustrated by Ashton's account of her and her partner's unexplained infertility (2008). There are many for whom the initial discovery or confirmation of their infertility comes as a devastating blow at the very time they thought they would be embarking on a pregnancy. Lucy, one of Black and Scull's respondents, describes being completely stopped in her tracks, as the news of the termination of her dreams of having a child 'goes straight through to the subconscious' (2005, p. 44). Some people, male and female, are in profound shock and may find the diagnosis impossible to believe. For some infertile individuals, the memory of their realisation of their condition is likely to remain indelibly imprinted into their brain.

Sharing the burden – or not

Couples

Even when the desire for parenthood is shared and a couple have a common cultural background, the experience of not being able to have children will not be identical for each partner and the impact on a relationship may be profound. Bentley comments on how men often seem conspicuous by their absence from discussions of infertility:

> *What makes it all even more difficult is that the whole area of infertility is so female-focused. Karen [his wife] and I joined the Infertility Network, but in the chatrooms it was the women who were chatting; the men were silent.* (2008, p. 3)

Even for couples such as Susan and Andrew (see Appendix 3), with a close, supportive relationship, there is the stress of seeing the other in pain or forced to undertake demeaning and even risky procedures, while the loss of spontaneity in people's sex lives can sometimes threaten a relationship.

As stated earlier, there are particular challenges for a couple to face if only one partner is infertile. An infertile man or woman is likely to feel guilt at preventing a fertile partner from having children, as will anyone who has already had children in another relationship. There may be much sadness and guilt between partners if the option of trying for a pregnancy could have been taken up earlier, when the chances of success might have been greater.

Wider family

There is a family loss, which may be felt deeply by would-be grandparents and other relatives. Knowing the consequences, some people with infertility problems will seek to carry their own anxieties and disappointments alone for as long as possible, while others will take their family with them and rely on their support in these difficult times. Even in the latter case, there can still be discomfort or even pain for all concerned when siblings, with whom much of life's journey has been shared, announce a pregnancy. Such matters are handled differently in different family cultures. Black and Scull's respondent, Linda, is Jewish:

> *As Jewish kids, you're brought up to succeed, to succeed in everything and anything you do . . . That's part of you . . . And so if what you want is six children then you're expected to have those six children . . . failure isn't part of the game.* (2005, p. 127)

Sue, by contrast, was brought up as a Roman Catholic and sees herself as burdened with a Catholic sense of guilt:

> *So if you're not blessed with children, then that's God punishing you for being guilty, or being bad. So you're constantly having this reiteration of your guilt.* (2005, p. 127)

Friends and colleagues

There is an impact, too, on friends and colleagues. Each pregnancy in the social circle is a painful reminder of infertility. Some, sensitive to their friends' troubles, may be hesitant about sharing their own delight with them. There is a risk that the ease will go out of valued friendships when they are no longer felt to be between equals. Some of Black and Scull's respondents felt a conspiracy of silence which meant there was never a right time to talk to others about their problem and feelings. One respondent found that this even applied when talking to childless friends:

> *I think that I've never had a completely honest conversation on both sides with any of my friends in that situation. I think there's a little bit of me that just doesn't want to say to anyone, 'Well, actually this has been a really big deal for me, and it's been really upsetting.' I think it's been the same thing for them as well, there's been a little bit of keeping up appearances on all sides.* (2005, p. 147)

Living through the ordeal

It would be a mistake to suppose that life for people undergoing fertility investigations and treatment is unremittingly bleak. It is usual for people to try to exercise control over their situation in whatever way they can, though this may often prove difficult. Couples commonly invest enormous energy and enterprise in giving treatment its best chance, as Susan's diary demonstrates (Appendix 3). Susan's husband, Andrew, in his own commentary, speaks of their determination to make IVF work; his investment in learning about the science behind the procedures; their careful and focused preparation for each cycle of treatment. He writes of pleasant clinics and supportive work colleagues, which made the process easier for them. Others have experienced sensitive and helpful fertility counselling. Nor is everyone engulfed in a round of treatment: some may decide to give themselves space between treatments or cope by maintaining as much of their normally enjoyable life as possible and keeping their treatment secret to themselves.

Grief

Grief can be felt at any time from the first suspicion of infertility to the conclusion of treatment and afterwards as, after the first shock of diagnosis, hopes and fears about infertility can seesaw repeatedly. Those who later proceed to adoption have had to face the ultimate failure of their enterprise. For some, there may be the added distress of having had to call a halt to treatment for medical, financial or other reasons rather than from a conviction that it would never be successful.

Rockel and Ryburn see grief as inescapable:

Grief is an unavoidable part of coming to terms with infertility. Like people suffering any other major loss, infertile couples may find that their grieving passes through a number of stages, sometimes moving backwards and forwards between them before it is resolved. (1988, p. 117)

Rawlings and Looi point out that because, for many people, there is no absolute certainty that they will not be able to have a child:

The usual picture of grief, of the single event which triggers the beginning, middle and "end" of an adjustment to loss really does not fit so well with the experience of fertility problems. (2007, p. 26)

The course of grief will also differ for people according to their personalities and circumstances, though all the stages listed above are likely to make an appearance. Grief may be profound so that sufferers become emotional or distracted and difficult to relate to, with consequences for family, friends and in the workplace. Some people may try hard to maintain an outwardly normal life but grief is still likely to take its toll, if only within the intimacy of a couple's relationship.

Denial

For some people who have known in advance of their infertility, this could mean a shelving of the issue for later consideration when the time for having children becomes urgent, or the right partner appears. To others for whom the need to have children is immediate and urgent, it may mean a refusal to believe the diagnosis or that treatment will be unsuccessful, whatever the medical evidence to the contrary. Many will have their moments of unrealistic confidence that a pregnancy is just around the corner, or of convincing themselves that having children is not so important after all. These are all normal initial human reactions to a situation which might otherwise feel intolerable but can sometimes seem to others to be carried to excess.

Pain and anger

Anger and despair are often described by those who later go on to adopt.

So the big question is, what do you do about it when you finally realise that you can't have children? Apart from scream, that is. And holler. And bawl your heart out to all and sundry. Then you might get bitter. You might have strong feelings of anger, self-pity and think, 'Why me?'. You will undoubtedly feel as if a knife has gone through you every time a friend or colleague tells you they are pregnant. I know I did. (James, 2006, pp. 2–3)

At this stage, it can feel difficult for friends and relatives to be of any help, especially family members experiencing their own grief.

Depression and sadness

The acute sense of loss of expectations and hopes described above may be succeeded by a longer-term sadness and yearning for what might have been. Again, it is not unrealistic or unreasonable for people to feel that the joy has gone out of their lives for a period, even after the acute edge has worn off their grief. The whole emotional and physical experience of infertility and treatment can be hugely exhausting, so it is hardly surprising if the body demands a period of quiescence, in which individuals can feel very flat in mood and generally depressed. Bentley, who is grateful for the ongoing support of his wife, nonetheless writes:

Rather than talk about it I found myself internalising the guilt and the shame and anger . . . It was certainly a test of our marriage and there have been some dark times when I would just go quiet and withdraw. (2008, p. 3)

Recovery and moving on

Surviving

> [The social worker] was sent, apparently, to ensure that we were not still "grieving" about IVF failures and infertility. What a stupid idea. I would never lose this sadness, this deep regret. But I was learning to live with it; we both were. (Ashton, 2008, p. 47)

People grieve differently and survival strategies in emotionally and physically stressful times also vary from person to person. Individually, an emotionally robust person is likely to be able to survive, whilst a personal background of trauma, abuse or neglect can leave someone weakened and without adequate emotional strategies to tackle the sort of stresses that infertility brings. Many infertile couples emphasise how the stresses upon themselves and their partners have served to demonstrate the strength of their relationship, whilst many others say that theirs has deepened and matured in the face of adversity. A good partnership bolsters self-esteem, which is in itself an important aid to surviving difficult times.

The chart *Pathways to Adoption* (see Appendix 2) contrasts 'internalised/expressive grieving' with 'externalised grieving'. The chart is helpful in drawing attention to the fact that there is no one way of coping and no blueprint for people to follow. At their extremes, neither of these models would assist recovery from the traumas of infertility. Black and Scull (2005, p. 175) draw an important distinction between avoiding the pain by 'containing and segregating' it, 'allowing us to get on with our lives in a reasonably functional way' (what one of their respondents described as deciding 'to put it in a box and just pop it up on a shelf and continue on with life'), and reaching a more profound resolution.

Taking back control

Some people are successful in maintaining a sense of control during diagnosis and treatment but, sadly, this is not always the case. Regaining command of one's own life then becomes of paramount importance in moving on. Rockel and Ryburn note that there are many ways to achieve this.

> Getting off the treatment merry-go-round can be a great relief. Making plans – for a trip, a job change, further education – is another way to take back control. Some also find that new friendships, with those who know about their infertility from the outset, can help with the

problem of other people's hopes and expectations. (1988, p. 121)

Writers on infertility stress the importance of restoring control over one's life after perhaps years in the hands of the medical profession. For many infertile people, this will ultimately mean drawing a line under treatment. It can be hard to disengage while there is still the chance of a pregnancy and some find this impossible but the relief at having made the decision can be restorative. Some deliberately pre-empt that feeling by deciding not to enter into treatment in the first place and, for them, this can feel a very positive choice.

"Alternative nurturing"

Black and Scull promote what they describe as 'alternative nurturing' as an aid to recovery, seeing this as encompassing a range of strategies to find new sources of pleasure and self-esteem. This might include involving oneself in other people's children or even adoption, but at the other extreme it might mean wholeheartedly embracing an alternative life which is free of dependents. They point out that there are many ways of looking after things and people other than caring for children. For Susan and Andrew in Appendix 3, it meant both deciding to adopt and, in the interim, making the most of the freedom of childlessness while they could. They write that they had 'an amazing time'.

ISSUES AND TASKS FOR SOCIAL WORKERS

- Recognise that infertility will have affected applicants physically and emotionally and that people may respond very differently.

- Gain some understanding of how applicants have coped with its complex stresses.

- Draw careful, well-evidenced conclusions about where applicants are in relation to their infertility, taking account of background factors such as education and culture.

- Be clear with enquirers and applicants that adoption is not a cure for infertility.

- Do not forget that moving on to adoption may not be appropriate for every infertile individual.

- Use the information you have gathered as a source of valuable evidence about how applicants deal with stress and function as a couple.

KEY MESSAGES

- Infertility is traumatic for most people, involving the loss of hopes and expectations of parenthood.

- It affects individuals, couples, their families and social networks.

- Undergoing treatment is likely to be physically and emotionally challenging.

- Most people are likely to experience grief, although they may deal with it in different ways.

- Most people come to terms with their infertility, at least to a degree, and embrace alternative ways of life.

5 Adoption

This chapter looks briefly at adoption as it is today. It is intended as a reminder of the gap that may well exist between applicants' understanding of adoption and current realities. We look at the following:

- adoption past and present;
- children who need adoption today;
- some issues for infertile adopters;
- adoptive parenthood.

Adoption past and present

History

Adoption has a very long history and means different things in different societies and cultures across the world. Although there have been societies in which adults have been adopted, it has normally been a formal or informal arrangement whereby children who need them acquire new parents to bring them up. As a legal procedure in Britain, it is less than a hundred years old and has undergone significant changes during this time. One reason why clarity is needed about what adoption is today is that public perceptions of it are partly coloured by what it used to be but is no longer. Another is that adoption, as understood in Britain, may be a very different arrangement for looking after children in need of permanent care than that prevalent in the country of origin of some of today's adopters.

Earlier purposes of adoption

From the early days of British adoption came the concepts of:

- giving a life-opportunity to children born into poverty, deprivation and sometimes moral degradation;
- removing the stigma of illegitimacy.

In the middle years of the twentieth century, adoption was also seen increasingly as a service for infertile couples and a complete transfer of parenthood. The door was closed against any further contact with the birth family although, eventually, adopters were encouraged to tell their children about their adoptive status.

In the 1950s and 1960s, adoption had become almost entirely a placement service for young, healthy and relinquished infants and for infertile couples. Mid-century was the era of "the perfect child for the perfect family". Consequently, some children were regarded as unadoptable and some applicants failed to meet exacting agency criteria relating to age, marital status, income, religious faith, etc.

The permanence movement

In the 1970s and 1980s, when social change brought about a decline in the number of babies for adoption, the focus moved instead to the many children who were spending their entire childhood in foster care or children's homes. Adoption came to be seen no longer as a service for adults but as a way of providing lifelong parents and a secure home to *all* children who might benefit. Thus, the scope of adoption widened to include:

- black children and those of mixed ethnicity;
- children with disabilities and additional health needs;
- older children, including some who had spent many years in public care.

Children who need adoption today

The move away from the infant adoptions of the mid-twentieth century is now almost total. Today's adopters are most likely to be in demand for:

- groups of two, three or even four or more siblings;
- children, often still very young, who have been exposed to parental drug and alcohol misuse, some before birth;
- older children from neglectful and abusive backgrounds;
- children whose ethnic make-up is complex;
- children with significant physical and mental disabilities;
- only a very few relinquished babies.

In all cases, some form of contact is likely to be maintained with children's birth families before and after an adoption order is granted. In Scotland, many of these children in need of adoption will be the subject of supervision requirements from the Children's Hearing system and will initially be placed on a fostering basis, so that their prospective adopters have a different legal standing until an adoption order is granted.

Issues for infertile adopters

Who can adopt?

Just as adoption is now offered to a much wider range of children than was the case 50 years ago, so a much wider range of adults is sought as adopters. In the past, some agencies had stringent criteria for accepting applications regarding employment, income, accommodation, etc, which are now regarded as less central. There remain, however, some basic legal requirements and agencies still have criteria of their own which they are legally required to make public. Examples of today's stipulations might include:

- infertility investigation and treatment has been completed;

- the oldest partner is no more than 40–45 years older than the child;

- in respect of younger children at least, that applicants should be non-smokers.

Extra tasks for adopters

A successful adoption should achieve for a child the secure, loving family life to which all parents aspire. There are, however, extra tasks required of adoptive families which have to be taken into account. A table of *Family Life Cycle Tasks of Adoptive Parents and Adopted Children* is reproduced in Appendix 1 (Brodzinsky *et al*, 1998, pp. 23–4). At its simplest, adoptive parents have to:

- undergo a formal assessment as a prospective "parent";

- reconcile themselves to the absence of conception, pregnancy and the process of birth;

- parent a child who is genetically different from themselves;

- care for a child who may be physically and emotionally damaged by earlier life experiences;

- receive "their" child from foster carers who may have been acting as the child's parents for some considerable time;

- manage contact with their child's birth family;

- explain adoption and share information with their child about his or her history and origins, possibly over years.

A change of focus: meeting the needs of a child

Veterans of infertility treatment find themselves entering a different world when they approach adoption and may be taken aback by this realisation. Cousins and Morrison note the irony that, whilst fertility counsellors may know little of adoption, adoption workers may have little experience of the fertility process, so that 'the two worlds, in essence so similar, are poles apart' (2003, p. 13). Enquirers will experience a change of focus. The processes and procedures of adoption are revealed as:

- children-centred;

- bureaucratic;

- aimed at preparing adults to undertake the tasks listed above.

In the world of fertility treatment, the service, including the counselling service, is:

- adult-centred;

- medical;

- aimed at a pregnancy and the subsequent birth of a healthy infant.

Openness about the fact that one or both parents of the baby may not be the biological parent is a recent development, not universally welcomed.

As Cousins and Morrison comment, 'the contrast is stark; the emotional switch is enormous' (2003, p. 12). It is therefore important that applicants take time to adjust. Those who have had previous personal contact with adopters or adopted people, or are adopted themselves, may have a head start in considering whether adoptive parenthood is right for them. Others may need much time to mull it over and partners will not always be in the same place in their thinking. This may not be welcome news to those who feel an undue amount of time has already gone by in their quest for parenthood.

A fresh start

The usual request of adoption agencies that infertility investigations and treatment should be finished can present a dilemma which is hard to resolve, especially for older enquirers. An adoption worker points out to enquirers that:

Both routes [to parenthood] are really hard emotionally and it's better not to be pulled in different directions. Better to take time to sort out which is the better route for you. (Personal communication)

For some people, however, the fresh start will come as a relief and trigger a surge of optimism. As an adoption worker comments, one person is often the focus of treatment but adoption is:

Something they can do together. For the first time, they are both in the same place. They want to get started . . . want control over the process and to do what they can to make parenting a reality – put themselves forward, be proactive. (Personal communication)

People anxious to take back control over their own lives after treatment can find this new focus dismaying and some will, themselves, come to an early conclusion that adoption is not for them. If, at an early stage, applicants have to be discouraged by the agency from proceeding further, it is important for workers to emphasise that this does not imply that they could not have made good parents to a birth child of their own. Otherwise, their sense of themselves as failures will be further, and unnecessarily, underlined.

Adoptive parenthood

Carer or parent?

Those who bring up an adoptive family are seen variously as:

- "carers", who bring someone else's child up to adulthood, within the security of an adoption order;

- "parents", on whom the courts have conferred parenthood of the child (in the words of the former Adoption Act 1976 s.39) 'as if he had been born as a child of the marriage';

- something in between.

Adoption's success as a way of providing a secure home for children has depended substantially on adopters' own wish to be "real" parents and to make a lifelong commitment to children they regard as their own. This has been particularly true of those who adopt after infertility, who hope to enter at last into their dream of being a "normal" family. Adopters have reported their delight in the simplest manifestations of ordinary life:

The best thing for me has been joining the other dads, pushing the buggy through the village on a Sunday morning. (Adoptive father, personal communication)

Many have been proud to talk of their adoptive children as "mine".

A different kind of "normality"

It could be said that an assumption of "normal" parenthood is merely an illusion and ignores important realities about life with today's adoptive children. Nonetheless, another adoptive parent makes a pertinent point:

An adopter's focus on "normal family life" may be artificial, but it is one that is usually encouraged, or at least not discouraged, by the professionals with whom adopters work. After all, "normal family life" is what children who need to be adopted need. (May, 2005, p. 71)

He also, somewhat ruefully, comments:

Prospective adoptive fathers are often hungry for the changes their children will produce in their lives. They crave the meaning family brings to our lives . . . some may be disappointed when they find family life is not solely composed of cherishable moments and therefore might benefit from having their expectations lowered in advance of placement. (p. 69)

Archer and Gordon confirm the warning:

The lives of children and their adoptive families are complex and multifaceted. The majority of children now placed for adoption have experienced damaging levels of traumatic separation, loss, neglect, abuse or inconsistent care that falls well short of Bowlby's concept of "good enough parenting". Their attachment patterns are insecure and disorganised: a variety of therapeutic inputs are frequently needed, for child, parents and family. (2006, p. 11)

It is to the credit of today's adoptive families that, with good preparation and support, they are ready to throw themselves heartily into being good parents to their children, to do their best to repair the damage inflicted by their previous experience – and to do it with love and delight, accepting their lives together as a different sort of "normality":

> *It's too tempting to see adoption as a situation that permanently colours a family's attitudes, staining any rose-tinted spectacles grey . . . Without trying to diminish the importance of such topics as abuse and attachment difficulties, we must also cheer loudly for the good things in family life – the good that triumphs over the early evil and misfortune that affects some children's lives.* (May, 2005, p. 69)

For those who choose to pursue adoption, however, neither an overemotional nor a tightly emotionally constrained temperament would prove helpful to the children Archer describes. Walker stresses that it is necessary for adopters to have 'resolved any losses and traumas in their own lives' (2008, p. 49). He also draws attention to the importance of adoptive parents having learned 'the ability to manage a wide range of feelings, both in themselves and others' – something which should have been done in early childhood, within the context of a securely attached relationship, 'through repeated interactions with primary carers who are able to help the infant or child to re-establish equilibrium and calm when distressed and upset'. Reflecting on these requirements in the light of the experience of infertility and its impact on their emotions should give would-be adopters and their assessing social workers ample food for thought and discussion. An examination of the applicants' coping mechanisms during this period would also be revealing. It would be unhelpful if these fell at the extremes of the *Pathways to Adoption* chart (see Appendix 2).

ISSUES AND TASKS FOR SOCIAL WORKERS

When first meeting enquirers, or responding to telephone enquiries, adoption workers should understand and acknowledge:

- the stresses that infertile people wishing to be parents have already experienced;
- the importance and difficulty of moving to a decision to embark on an adoption application;
- the need for time for recovery and reflection after fertility treatment before reinvesting their energies in adoption;
- the initial resentment of those enquirers who may see nothing wrong with embarking on an adoption application whilst still undergoing fertility treatment;
- the suspicion that some enquirers may feel about the adoption process and their anxiety about being devalued within it.

They should be familiar with:

- the most common causes of infertility;
- the experience of consultation, counselling and treatment offered by fertility clinics;
- the process of adoption;
- the needs of the children requiring adoptive placements;
- the assessment criteria of the agency.

They should provide:

- clear, accessible and accurate written and verbal information;
- an opportunity for private discussion at an early stage, especially if

there are any issues which enquirers feel may be an impediment to adoption, e.g. health, unsuitable accommodation, life changes, etc;

- suggestions for further reading and contacts for people to meet.

These matters are important in the early stages of applicants' contact with an adoption agency, enabling those who decide to pursue adoption to set out in good heart and those who decide it is not for them to be comfortable with their decision. Thereafter, they remain relevant to the whole process of adoption and all the work that workers and applicants undertake together.

KEY MESSAGES

- Adoption has changed drastically in the last 20 years in particular.

- The population of children needing adoptive families is comprised largely of children past infancy and those who have been exposed to early neglect or abuse.

- Contact with a child's birth family is now a feature of most adoptions.

- An adoption application is a new and very different enterprise from pursuing infertility treatment.

- Applicants need time and informed, supportive assistance to help them make the transition.

- Successful adopters are strongly motivated to be "normal" parents but need to acknowledge that their task as parents is different in important respects to that of birth parents and will make extra demands on them.

6 Assessment

Once embarked on a journey towards adoption, applicants have much to learn and to think about before their offer can be presented to an adoption panel. In this chapter, we consider the assessment processes undertaken by social workers with all applicants offering to provide any form of substitute family care. In particular, however, we concentrate on the issues to be explored when assessing infertile applicants. We examine:

- the concept of assessment;

- stages on the journey towards adoption;

- the home study and the principle of "evidence";

- how the issues arising from infertility might be explored in assessment;

- the dilemma of providing evidence of understanding/experience of children for childless applicants.

Assessment

Definition

In writing the chapter, we have defined "assessment" as the process of forming a view as to whether or not someone is capable of undertaking a specified task competently. In order to conduct an assessment, therefore, it is important that there is an understanding of the job to be done and the qualities necessary to do that job at least adequately.

Aims of assessment

Assessment has several aims. Primarily, the purpose is to enable and support confident decision-making based on comprehensive information, analysis and evaluation. During the process of assessment, it is hoped that applicants can come to a shared understanding with assessors about the requirements of the task and whether or not they can meet these requirements. In addition, there should be opportunities for applicants and assessors to enhance their understanding and values of the applicant's family life. In their publication, *Making Good Assessments*, Barker *et al* write that:

Anyone applying to care for other people's children, whether by fostering or by adoption,

needs both the opportunity to learn about the tasks and the skills required and also the space to reflect on what it will mean for themselves as individuals and as families. There is a balance to be struck between the educative, task-centred, skills-development approach and the development of insight and self-awareness by applicants. (1999, p. 5)

A journey towards adoption

Applicants for adoption who have seen themselves as being on a "journey" through infertility may see their progress towards adoption as a continuation of the same journey, or the beginning of an entirely new one. Social workers stress the differences between adoption and having children by birth, particularly in light of the many challenges brought by today's adoptive children. They favour a pause for reflection after the end of fertility treatment and the sense of a clean break and a new endeavour. An experienced adoption social worker, struck by how often her applicants adhere to the notion that adoption is simply a continuation of one long journey towards parenthood, has suggested that a better way of looking at it would be to think in terms of a single "two-flight journey". Of the many who enquire about adoption but withdraw on discovering that adopting is not a simple matter of acquiring a young, healthy baby similar to one who might have been born to them, she writes:

They might be said to have been on the first flight, or first leg, of their parenting journey through the fertility treatments and to have landed in disappointment. From there, it might be said that they take the next flight back home after attending an information evening. There is no pretending for the couples who adopt babies today that he/she could be the child born to them. (Personal communication)

Those who do proceed towards adoption, she prefers to think of as suffering the pain of *childlessness* rather than *infertility*, a significant distinction:

Adoptive parents are those who make the first landing in disappointment and recover enough to proceed on to the next leg of their parenting journey by taking the second flight through the adoption process. It is the longing to be a parent and the pain of childlessness that drives them forward. These are the ones whose need to parent has allowed them to consider parenting someone else's child. From there, it is hoped that the adoption training and assessment process opens their hearts and minds to the needs of the adopted child for loving and sensitive parents, so that the adopters and the child both have their needs met. The best adopters are the ones who can go on to put the needs of the child uppermost in this equation. (Personal communication)

Stages on the journey

Just as infertile adopters might be viewed as travellers, the preparation and assessment process itself might also be viewed as a journey with several stages or themes.

Information gathering

This is broadly equivalent to checking in and passing through Security and is usually carried out at an initial stage.

- Necessary information is specified primarily by law and regulations.

- Statutory health checks, references and checks for criminal offences are carried out.

- These are designed to "screen" applicants in order to protect vulnerable children.

- Information on an applicant's life experience and history will be a necessary base for evaluation of potential parenting capacity and the ability to undertake adoption tasks.

Preparation

Having boarded the flight, information is then given to passengers before the flight actually begins. To assist that process, most adoption agencies run preparation groups, usually as a precursor to assessment and often following a set curriculum, such as that offered in *Preparing to Adopt* (Beesley *et al*, 2006). Unlike in-flight information, which is short-term, preparation courses are designed to provide a useful guide for adopters over the years ahead. Most preparation courses:

- provide information on the children who require adoption today;

- address issues such as attachment, separation and loss, contact and parenting strategies;

- allow applicants the opportunity to consider whether adoption feels right for them;

- are a rich source of learning and also of evidence for the assessment itself.

Sharing the experience of infertility

Preparation courses are enriched when applicants feel comfortable enough to share experiences with each other as part of the learning process. This has to be very sensitively handled by the workers running the groups. Thus, Ashton writes:

I was relieved that there were no revelations about endless IVF treatment, miscarriages and broken hearts and dreams during the sessions. Some of that would come out over friendly lunches and quiet coffee breaks. (2008, p. 54)

An adoption worker stresses, in particular, the vulnerability of infertile applicants exchanging personal information during the introductory session of a course and the importance of emphasising that "brief personal details" really means just that:

It is so easy for people to fall into telling the whole story of their infertility and for it to be relayed back to the group, often to the dismay of a partner who might not be comfortable with it having been discussed at all. The trouble is, it's what's in their heads. (Personal communication)

One key message of preparation groups is that loss lies at the core of adoption. It is an experience shared by all sides of the "adoption triangle". Courses often put emphasis on this shared experience and encourage applicants to think of the usefulness of their own experiences of loss and grief, including those arising from their infertility, in helping their adopted child. This is sensitive work, especially as preparation groups may be composed of applicants considered most likely to meet the needs of the children on referral, rather than those chosen for their compatibility with each other.

Referring to the session where grief and loss are explored, the same worker goes on to stress the importance of taking care of peoples' feelings, whatever their experience of loss; in particular, for those to whom it is applicable, when sharing any details of their experience of infertility.

Warn them beforehand and ask them to talk to partners about what to share and what not. Put them into single gender groups. The guys will say they will just get up-to-date on the football but in the home study, they will tell you it was the first time they had talked about it to anyone outside. For some people, it can be hard but it can also be quite liberating. They may find they can share in a group some of the stuff they have not been able to talk about with their families and they are able to explore how that feels. It is also a first opportunity to get over the message that those losses are not going to go away and this is a start of reminding them of this. Don't ask for personal feedback! (Personal communication)

Part of this discussion will centre on coping strategies which applicants have found worked for them and what things made them feel particularly vulnerable. People are understandably wary of revealing vulnerability and need to know that this is as essential to success in adoption as building on their existing strengths.

Home study

At this point, applicants may consider themselves to be "mid-flight" in the second stage of the journey to parenthood.

Most adoption agencies conduct assessments using one or two social workers who will have a series of planned meetings with the applicant during which necessary information will be gathered and there will be a discussion on a range of topics surrounding adoption.

- Applicants will be expected to contribute to this process by providing information, carrying out exercises and providing written reflection on what they have learned.

- Honest, reflective discussion needs to take place to help applicants think themselves into the reality of what it will be like to care for a child not born to them.

- A central area in the assessment of infertile applicants should be the whole issue of infertility and the degree to which the surrounding emotions have been confronted and resolved.

- The home study must contain an element of analysis, indicating how the worker has interpreted the information collated and arrived at an ultimate recommendation.

Competence-based assessments

In recent years, there has been an attempt to set out the core components of the adoption task as "competencies", required by substitute parents. While some adoption workers have voiced discomfort with

this approach, it can be a useful way of highlighting the substantiating factors which support the ultimate recommendation.

Part 4 of BAAF's *Form F* sets out the five competencies considered necessary for adopters. In many assessments it has been found helpful for applicants and assessors to identify what they consider to be relevant evidence for these specified competencies. Often the applicants will also compile a portfolio to provide further evidence of their competencies.

- A competence-based approach to assessment can clarify and reinforce the nature of the task to be undertaken.

- It can provide a clear, agreed set of criteria against which the applicant is measured.

- It affirms the importance of skills and knowledge gained by the applicant throughout life and in a wide variety of situations, a factor of particular relevance to infertile applicants whose direct experience of children may be limited.

- It allows the applicant and assessor to identify legitimate gaps in the applicants' knowledge and to agree a strategy for addressing these.

- By allowing the applicant to compile a portfolio, it can transfer some control to the applicant, thereby addressing some of the power imbalance which can be inherent in assessments.

- In essence, it breaks activities down into functions and is concerned with what can be demonstrated, is observable and measurable.

Providing evidence

Evidence consists of those factors which the worker and the applicant contend are demonstrable proof of the applicant's ability to discharge a certain function. In the past, many assessments have done little more than indicate that infertile applicants 'have grieved for their loss and come to terms with it'. While this may well be the case, assessors need to be able to spell out why they consider this to be so.

There are two particular areas where infertile applicants will be called upon to provide evidence:

- that they have sufficiently processed powerful emotions which may have emanated from their inability to reproduce.

- that they possess an understanding and an appreciation of children's needs, particularly the likely needs of children requiring adoptive placements.

Evidence of resolution of feelings associated with infertility

We have already suggested that it is not uncommon for both applicants and assessors to regard the experience of infertility as a kind of bereavement, where hopes of parenthood are lost. Even if the infertile adopters' experience can also be regarded as a journey, the concept of loss and grief cannot be completely jettisoned. Determining the point which individuals have reached can be assisted by an understanding of the progress of grieving, as outlined in Chapter 4. In discussion and written descriptions, it is possible to identify the point at which people have arrived. This can be done by:

- examining the coherence of the narrative;
- considering the vocabulary used;
- noting the presence or absence of emotion;
- checking with relatives and referees.

It is important, however, to re-emphasise the message from earlier chapters that, just as adopters are all different in personality and experience, neither should infertility be inferred to mean the same for all adopters. A clear reason for failing to conceive probably means that a reasonable parallel can be made between the journey to adoption and the process of grieving. In fact, some people may have experienced specific episodes of loss such as miscarriages or even a stillbirth and will have gone through a process of mourning following those events. Many people, however, come to adoption with unexplained infertility, a residual chance of conceiving, as a gay or lesbian couple or a single applicant. Some couples simply find that they have left it too late to conceive, albeit that they may technically be fertile. All these people may come to adoption with a different attitude to the process and the assessment. Some individuals, moreover, externalise their grief and it is the people in the above categories and who externalise their grief whom social workers can find the most difficult to assess (see Appendix 2).

A coherent narrative

Applicants can be asked to give an account, perhaps confirmed in writing, of their experience of infertility. The ability to present a coherent narrative is evidence in itself that the applicants have gained some perspective on their experience. There is a parallel with attachment theory and the importance of "organised" states of mind with respect to attachment in an Adult Attachment Interview (Main *et al*, 2008, p. 32). For one adoption worker, the question is:

Can the person produce a reasonably coherent, concise and relevant story of the event and "make sense" of it in a way that does not involve excessive anger, guilt or blame? (Personal communication)

Another adoption worker stresses the importance of hearing the whole story.

We need a real strong sense of where the individual has been, how they supported each other as a couple and where their support came from in terms of friends and family. All this will be relevant for how they cope in the future as adoptive parents. (Personal communication)

Social workers must, however, bear in mind that applicants' ability to present their story coherently will be influenced by their skills and experience in self-presentation. It is not so much a polished account that is needed so much as a narrative that has a clear meaning for the applicants themselves.

Messages from childhood

As mentioned in Chapter 5, Walker (2008) summarises three important aspects that any assessment of potential substitute carers should address:

- the ability to manage a wide range of feelings both in themselves and others;
- the resolution of any losses or traumas that they have experienced in their lives;
- the acquisition of a reflective function.

These attributes will often have their roots in an individual's secure childhood and positive experience of parenting. Assessors can find it useful to explore with applicants how the highs and lows of family childhood experiences which the applicants themselves have identified were managed. A mature, objective consideration of one's childhood, recognising its influence on oneself, can clearly demonstrate that reflective function is well developed.

Vocabulary

Vocabulary, of itself, is not a completely reliable indicator of the individual's resolution of the feelings surrounding infertility. The topic under discussion is emotive and painful and the words used can be strong and emotive, too. Nevertheless, a consistent use of the past tense, the description of the investigation and treatment, of major events such as miscarriages or terminations, the positive language used to convey how the decision to move on was reached, can all provide clues to the individual's inner state and capacity to regulate emotion. The tone of voice, body language and appropriate humour can all complement or contradict the vocabulary, although it should be stressed that subjective assessments must be avoided and assessors must cultivate skills of objective observation.

Emotion

The feelings which are likely to predominate at the various stages of the grieving process have already been detailed in Chapter 4 and assessors need to interpret the emotions which they encounter during the home study. In essence, both applicants and their worker need to identify evidence that the applicants have now accommodated the losses inflicted by infertility and are moving on with self-esteem and a sense of self-worth reasonably intact. Often, it is a matter of degree and whilst some anger, regret, sadness or tears are to be expected, intense outpourings of resentment, despair and frustration may well indicate that applicants are not in a "safe place" emotionally and that adoption is not yet a realistic option.

Applicants can be asked to give their reasons why they think the strong feelings engendered by infertility have been processed and are now well regulated. Quick's suggested *Pathways to Adoption* referred to above (Appendix 2) and Exercise 2 in Appendix 4 are useful tools. Both applicants and worker may find these helpful benchmarks as they seek to ascertain the information which can be reasonably interpreted as meaning that the intense, pervasive emotions have been sufficiently subdued to allow the individual to deal with life and to approach adoption in good emotional shape.

The importance of being able to handle all strong emotions and its relevance to helping children damaged by their life experiences is made by Walker, who also stresses carers' importance as role models for their children:

> *An assessment of substitute carers, therefore, will need to focus on the individual's capacity to be in touch with a range of feelings in him/herself. It will be important that the individual can experience feelings of joy and*

happiness as well as sadness and hurt. This ability to be comfortable with a whole range of feelings will enable the carer to remain emotionally regulated him or herself in the face of the child's strong, often provocative, feelings. (2008, p. 50)

Relatives and referees

Referees, family members, general practitioners and members of support groups which applicants may have used during their journey, can all give collaborative evidence on how an individual has processed the issues arising from infertility. In all attempts to set out evidence to support a recommendation, the assessor is seeking to establish congruence and if partners describe things similarly, if referees say that is how it was, if applicants talked in similar tones in preparation groups, if they have behaved in like fashion in other, parallel situations, then it is reasonable to conclude that that is how they are in reality.

Homework

We have included some further specific exercises intended to allow people to explore infertility in assessments in Appendix 4. In some instances, completed exercise sheets may be shared with the assessor; in other cases, it may be more appropriate for individuals to examine the issues raised on their own or with a partner. It is not intended that assessors should intrude unduly into sensitive, extremely private areas but it is important that some understanding is gained of the individual's reaction to infertility. A man still nursing fears and anxieties about his perception of his manhood, a woman still preoccupied with thoughts of her own lack of wholeness, may have difficulties in forming a bond with a non-biologically related child, the tangible evidence of another man's potency and of another woman's fecundity.

Evidence of a knowledge of children

This can be extremely difficult for childless applicants to provide. There will be obvious situations where individuals have relevant professional experience or qualifications and others where applicants have extensive exposure to children within their family and social network or via sporting and leisure pursuits. Other applicants will have to rely on homework such as case studies, reading materials, etc, and discussions thereafter. Using such material, however, means the assessor must be clear about the sort of information he or she is attempting to elicit and must be prepared to examine a wide range of responses objectively.

Short-term experience

Occasionally, suggestions are made that individuals should seek more direct experience of children via children's organisations, respite fostering, helping at day care centres, etc. If such routes are to be followed, it is important to be absolutely clear about the evidence likely to be provided and how that will be recognised. The task of befriending or providing respite care, for example, is markedly different from that of adoption – there may not necessarily be parallels and applicants may approach such undertakings in a very different frame of mind. As emphasised earlier, it is essential to think creatively about applicants' whole situation and background since, even in areas of their life where children did not feature, there can be clear similarities with the specific elements of the adoption task.

Using adopters' experience

A number of agencies try to ensure that an experienced adopter helps to lead the preparation group or, at least, is a contributor in one or two sessions. Others may link applicants with seasoned adopters at some point during the home study. While this practice must have clear parameters to protect privacy and confidentiality, this can be a useful vehicle for exposing adopters to the reality of caring for someone else's children. Furthermore, it can provide a focus for discussion as both assessor and childless applicants endeavour to establish an understanding of children's needs.

Other relevant aspects

Not all evidence relating to the applicants' ability to care for a child needs to come from quantifying the frequency and nature of their contacts with children. An adoption worker writes:

A key subject in the home study is an applicant's ability to accept difference and to believe that "different doesn't mean bad". I would look for evidence in how the applicants talk about children; not having stereotypical views about what they'd expect; an ability to talk to/and about children being different from themselves; not expecting replicas of themselves but being realistic and explicit about what would be OK in their particular family. And I would look for evidence that they were open to learning.
(Personal communication)

It must also not be forgotten that all applicants have themselves been children. They have experienced being brought up with adults and the ability to talk about and to reflect on that experience, identifying the needs which they experienced and the way in which they felt these needs to have been appropriately met, can also provide a great deal of relevant information. Many individuals will adopt parenting strategies which are broadly similar to those utilised by their parents. To examine why this is likely to happen, what are seen as the benefits or, conversely, to consider why applicants would wish to employ very different strategies, can also demonstrate a clear understanding of what children need and what does and does not work.

ISSUES AND TASKS FOR SOCIAL WORKERS

Acknowledge that:

- while the process is not intended to be intrusive, it is essential that full preparation for today's adoption tasks is undertaken;

- it is essential to work in partnership with applicants to enable them to be active in their own learning and preparation for adoption.

Help applicants:

- to think imaginatively and widely about their life experiences and the attributes that may have resulted from them;

- to collate evidence that they possess the abilities required to meet the tasks faced by adopters;

- to identify those factors which they consider have helped them overcome the pain and disappointment of infertility.

Remember that:

- assessing infertile applicants means exploring painful and intimate areas of people's lives;

- such assessment must be done with their co-operation and the assessing worker must be respectful;

- evaluating the information and demonstrating the way in which it has been used is essential.

KEY MESSAGES

- All assessment must contain an analytical element;

- The assessor and the applicants must indicate the way in which feelings associated with infertility have been confronted and resolved;

- Congruence in how applicants describe their journey, how they behave in a range of situations, how they are described and experienced by others, is strong, supportive evidence for any assessment.

Matching and placement

This chapter is concerned with the all-important period after applicants have been approved to adopt until a child is settled in with them. Completing the assessment, being presented to panel and ultimately being approved as adopters can feel like the end of a flight that was turbulent at times but which ended in a smooth, safe touch-down. In reality, however, the journey is not over and the long haul has yet to begin.

From approval to placement

Whilst this period is clearly not part of the assessment, it can still be a useful period of consolidation, when learning can be confirmed and even augmented. Now that the adopters have been approved, it is possible to revisit some topics in greater depth, to ask questions applicants did not feel able to ask during assessment and to continue preparations for the future. While the lack of resources may not always permit, a period of rest and recovery can produce adopters who are much better placed to continue the journey towards adoptive parenthood. This chapter covers the following:

- waiting;
- matching and meeting;
- placement and settling in.

Waiting

After applicants are approved, the dream of becoming a parent begins to come alive. This can be an exciting time but is just as likely to prove frustrating. This is so for all adopters who find themselves waiting months, or occasionally years, for a match with a child but is likely to be even more trying for infertile people for whom it seems an extension of an already long journey to parenthood.

It is a time when adopters have begun to take on their new identity as people worthy to care for a child but cannot yet begin to make any practical changes in their day-to-day lives. This will be especially difficult for people who have dealt with the earlier frustrations of infertility treatment by constantly planning ahead. Intercountry adopters often have an even more

difficult wait, in that their future as parents is in the hands of people in far-off places with whom they have no personal contact. Prospective adopters value a social worker who is in touch with them on a regular basis and who can be reliably contacted, if needed.

Matching and meeting

It can be difficult for prospective adopters to assimilate information about children for whom they might be suitable whilst dealing with their own excitement and impatience to move on, especially if this is coupled with a resurrection of old, painful feelings and a lingering desire for the child of their dreams. Even if discussed beforehand, the process of being matched with and meeting a child may occasion a renewed sense of the unfairness of infertility, the artificiality of becoming a parent through adoption and a renewed sense of inadequacy.

The last emotion may be especially the case if the adopters decline to be linked with a specific child with difficulties, or are not deemed equal to the task when a full exploration of a possible match takes place. Trusting their social worker to suggest only appropriate matches is a key component in helping prospective adopters through these critical discussions.

Particular difficulties arise for applicants in agencies which still suggest more than one family to a matching panel. The devastation of thinking yourself almost there as parents, only to hear that another family has been chosen, can lead to adopters failing to have their hearts and minds open when listening to details of subsequent children, as self-protection against further disappointment. People who have been through this process and been disappointed more than once may well withdraw, rather than suffer further rejections.

Letting go of the fantasy child

It is usual for all prospective parents to imagine the child they are going to have and the times they are going to have together. The arrival of an actual child, warts and all, either by birth or adoption, moves most people on to a new reality but Walker warns:

. . . if the imagined birth child has not been mourned, the danger is that this fantasised child will be idealised with the effect that the adoptive child will inevitably be a disappointment. (2008, p. 51)

With the "fantasy child" may disappear lingering hopes of a "fantasy lifestyle", however much applicants' hopes of sharing a specific passion with a child have been doused by a social worker during the home study. Cowling (undated) suggests that it can be helpful to adoptive parents to do some work to 'recognise what you want to pass down to your child so that you understand your expectations of family life'.

It is particularly important for a couple to keep checking with each other to make sure they are "in the same place" regarding a child under discussion. An experienced adoption worker warns of the need for vigilance in case the "fantasy child" is still about:

Sometimes it's a gender thing. People say they have no preference, but when a boy is offered and they seem unenthusiastic, they'll suddenly realise: 'I know now, it's a wee girl I want!'. Sometimes it comes out when thinking about names. They want to choose a name of their own for a child after all we've been through about accepting a child's birth name. It's about naming your child. Then I have encountered situations when one of a couple is fertile: when a child is offered, they come face to face with the fact that they could have a child with another partner – and the whole thing falls apart. (Personal communication)

Matching discussions

Matching discussions will focus on a child's:

- ethnicity and physical appearance;
- health and development;
- background history;
- personality;
- wishes and those of his or her parents.

Ethnicity and physical appearance

It is normal for families to claim their newly born babies by noting similarities to family members. Accepting that any likeness is accidental and not genetic may bring pangs of regret for adopters. Brebner *et al*, writing of new placements of very young babies, concluded that:

It seems that the perception of likeness is central to the adoptive family's sense of its own psychological identity. (1985, p. 38)

They observed ways in which their "baby" adopters' behaviour replicated that of any other parent, even showing a compulsion to fly in the face of reality by noting similarities between their own features and those of a newly arrived baby. They noted that:

On no occasion at this early stage of adoption did one hear the words or receive the impression 'The baby isn't like us'. (p. 38)

It is, of course, much more difficult for the prospective adopters of children past infancy to claim similarities but it may be equally difficult to acknowledge that they find a child under discussion physically unappealing. It is extremely important that they should be able to confess that they feel "the chemistry isn't right", rather than to let themselves be swept along into the placement.

In intercountry adoption, if the child is of a different race, adopters will, of course, have prepared themselves for being a family with a very public and visible difference but this, of itself, will not make them invulnerable to uncomfortable feelings. Researchers into intercountry adoption outcomes in Ireland also offer the following warning:

Parents . . . may be prone to a kind of racial stereotyping. We noted . . . that many of the little girls were described as "precious" or "a little doll" or "a little flower". Such epithets might be difficult for these children to live up to when they get a bit older and could also operate as a psychological straitjacket. (Greene *et al*, 2007, p. 345)

Health and development

During assessment, applicants will have been asked to consider children:

- who may have additional health needs;
- who have been exposed to early adversity;
- about whom there may be some developmental uncertainty.

The terms of their ultimate approval will have been carefully defined. In subsequent discussions about children needing placement, however, it can be tempting for social workers to respond over-enthusiastically to approved adopters' interest in a child whom they feel moved to help. In their excitement, adopters may not always hear the information which has been given and, even when it is provided in writing, may not fully take on board the possible short- and long-term implications. In their eagerness to get on with family-building, infertile adopters have more reason than others to underestimate the challenges ahead and may need help to keep a realistic perspective on their child. A consultation with the agency's medical adviser, with a subsequent written summary, is usually the best way to encourage a full exploration of issues of health and development.

Background history

Adopters will have been exposed to considerable information about the very difficult circumstances which result in children requiring adoptive families. They will have considered the impact of early adversity on children and their development and will have accepted this as part and parcel of adoption today.

When an actual child who might become their own is under discussion, however, the contrast between what might have been and what is now being offered is stark and can act as a trigger for applicants back to the pain and sadness of their own infertility. They may feel anger that their infertility obliges them to make painful choices about taking on potentially difficult situations, or indeed anger against birth parents who have harmed a child about to become their own. They may also be so eager to compensate for the child's hurt that they become over-optimistic about their own ability to repair earlier damage.

"Stretching"

The assessment process will ultimately have resulted in a clear recommendation, agreed by both adopters and assessor, on the most appropriate terms of approval for these applicants. The evidence in support of this will have been clearly set out in the assessment report and should not only illustrate the skills and attributes possessed by the prospective adopters but should also lead to a recommendation which is both logical and reasonable. It is vitally important, therefore, that workers, applicants and adoption panel members remind themselves of this when considering potential matches between children and approved adoptive families.

Whilst some growth and re-evaluation may have occurred in the period following approval, it is all too easy to be convinced that an extra child, a slightly older child, a child with a few additional needs, is not that far removed from the situations envisaged when the original recommendation was reached. Adopters,

knowing that a real child is imminently available at last, may be unable to remain focused on their own, legitimate hopes. Workers, confident about "their" family's ability and aware of their agency's placement needs, may become convinced that this match is perfectly suitable, even if not quite in line with the approval conditions. Workers should try to remember the journey made by infertile applicants, the losses and adjustments encountered en route, to ensure that, as far as possible, there is no major diversion to an unsuitable destination.

Placement and settling in

Lingering regrets

The days and weeks before, during and after a placement are usually extremely busy ones in which suddenly, after all the waiting, there is so much to be done. It is also a time when agencies are likely to be necessarily prescriptive about how and when introductions to the child proceed. The focus now is very much on the interaction between the adopters and the child who is to become theirs. A worker with a trusting relationship with the adopters may well be able to pick up and acknowledge signs of the lingering pain of infertility. However well concealed, the adopters might still be feeling:

- regret at the absence of a pregnancy and birth with their associated procedures and rituals;

- a lingering desire for the child of their dreams;

- a reluctance to use contraception (in cases of unexplained infertility) in order to avoid a pregnancy while a child settles in.

Family-building

Nowadays, new adopters are carefully schooled in the early days of adoptive family-building, with the adopters taking over the lead role in nurturing relationships with their children from whomever previously held this role (usually foster carers). To do this, they may have to hold at arms length, for a while, their wider family, who themselves have been eagerly awaiting the new arrival.

One of the advantages of meeting relatives during the assessment period is to help adopters prepare those closest to them to hold at bay their own instinct to rejoice that the long saga of infertility is at an end. Would-be grandparents may have felt many years of frustration and sadness at not being able to fulfil this role and are likely to feel alienated from the adoption process if they do not understand why they are initially being kept at a distance. As social workers are much less likely to be in attendance immediately after a child is brought from overseas, it is especially important that intercountry adopters are prepared to protect their new child from bombardment by eager and excited new relatives.

Experiencing symptoms of "postnatal blues" without a birth

On the face of it, this would seem a particularly surprising and unfair consequence of the much-awaited placement of a child. It is not, however, unusual for adopters to experience some of the ups and downs in mood usually associated with hormonal changes after a birth and sometimes people can find

themselves mourning the absence of birth children even as they put their energy into learning to parent the child who will be theirs through adoption. Fatigue can play a big role, as with all new parents who must adjust to a new and demanding way of life. Social workers can usefully discuss this with applicants during the home study, so that the adopters have made their plans for coping in advance. In Cowling's view, having "the blues" can be helpful:

This represents a mourning of the lost ideal. It can be seen not as a pathological symptom in the parent but as a positive form of adaptive grieving. This is a form of grieving when, at a later date, a person fully experiences the reality of their loss in a new way. (undated)

ISSUES AND TASKS FOR SOCIAL WORKERS

- Help adopters to pace themselves appropriately and not rush towards a placement prematurely.

- Keep in touch and remain sensitive to the impact infertility may continue to have on their feelings.

- Appreciate the emotional intensity of the period of matching, meeting and placement.

- Be cautious about "stretching" infertile adopters into situations for which they have not been specifically prepared in terms of the age range of child, more complex needs, sibling groups, etc.

- Bear in mind that the wider family has also experienced pain and grief as a result of the adopters' infertility.

KEY MESSAGES

- Adoption is not, of itself, an absolute and permanent resolution of infertility.

- Adopters and their families can often be subject to a resurgence of painful feelings arising from infertility when confronted with a real child.

- Adopters need the support of a trusted social worker so that these feelings are not submerged in the excitement of matching and the placement of a child.

- Relief, over-confidence and optimism must be guarded against by both workers and social workers at the point of matching.

Lifelong issues

This chapter is concerned with what Patricia Irwin Johnston (1992) calls 'infertility's aftershocks'. Adoption brings joy and a sense of purpose and achievement to many adoptive parents. Their children are deeply loved and valued and most grow up to be adults of whom their parents can be justly proud. Despite this, there will be occasions when the pain of infertility returns, sometimes as a brief, sharp stab, occasionally as a trigger for more prolonged distress and depression. Here, we also highlight some of the situations in which the strength gained from having come to terms with infertility can be utilised to help a child with their own challenges.

This chapter touches on the following:

- the continuing impact of infertility;
- sharing the child;
- the child in the adoptive family.

The continuing impact of infertility

Negative feelings

There are many aspects of life with adopted children which can be clouded by lingering feelings about infertility. Some of the negative feelings which may re-emerge include the following:

- grief, loss and sadness for the absence of birth children;
- feelings of failure and inadequacy;
- feelings of unfairness and jealousy;
- a feeling that adoption is second-best parenthood.

Positive feelings

It is important that such feelings, which may be powerful at times and very undermining, are balanced by feelings of strength and capacity, also gained from the experience of infertility. These might include:

- the knowledge that you have survived difficult times;
- increased empathy for others in difficulty;

- confidence in the tried and tested support of a partner or of close friends and relatives;
- confidence in the adoption agency and its ongoing support.

Most importantly:

- a strong sense of being your child's parent with all the authority that parenthood commands.

An experienced social worker, reflecting that many who have experienced the pain of infertility move on to make successful adopters, comments:

What these people carry forward from the infertility process is self-awareness. They have been able to recover from the pain of the child not born to them, and find delight and reward in parenting an adopted child. They are the ones who can suspend their gratification until the child is ready to say 'I love you' and really mean it because they have found satisfaction in parenting a child who needs them. Hitting the bottom of the grief process and coming up again has allowed them to give something of themselves to the child, that has its own rewards, it enhances their self-esteem. (Personal communication)

Anniversaries and personal milestones

Times associated with acute feelings of grief and loss are not, however, easily forgotten. Anniversaries associated with a journey through infertility will continue to be remembered with pain, for example:

- the diagnosis of infertility;
- the beginning or end of a treatment cycle;
- a miscarriage or termination;
- a stillbirth.

Life is also punctuated by personal milestones for the adopter, as for every adult. These might include:

- reaching the menopause;
- the death of one's own parents;
- being widowed;

- becoming dependent on one's children in old age.

The process of ageing will, in many cases, underline the loving and ever-maturing relationship that adoptive parents have with their children. Some people, though, become more distanced from their children in adulthood. This may well rekindle feelings of failure and nurture a fantasy that a genetic child would have been emotionally closer and maybe even of more practical help.

Stages of parenthood

Adopters are as keen as anyone to experience the rituals of parenthood but these may be tinged with regret for the child who was never born to them. Depending on the age of children at placement, any of the following may give rise to unexpected pain:

- gatherings of parents of babies and toddlers, at which reminiscences of pregnancy and birth are frequent;

- the birth of children to siblings, relatives and friends;

- a return to work after adoption leave;

- the milestones in an adoptive child's life, especially birthdays;

- having to explain to your little child that he or she was not "in this mummy's tummy";

- a first day at nursery or school;

- schoolwork for a child involving "families" or sex education;

- leaving home;

- getting married;

- the birth of a first grandchild, especially if an adopted daughter is very young, or there are concerns about her ability to be a good parent;

- an adopted son or daughter experiencing fertility problems.

An adopter stresses the way in which these milestones can trigger a throwback to earlier feelings:

When my granddaughter was born, I was thrilled but also saddened. She was mine but once again not mine. I was delighted when my daughter became pregnant, but conscious that this was not an experience I had ever shared. (McMillan and Irving, 1999, p. 7)

Sharing the child

One of the central tasks of adoptive parenthood is to share children with their birth families. At a minimum, this will involve helping children to know their adoption story. At the other end of the spectrum, it could mean maintaining a face-to-face relationship with another family, over many years. This time it is not only the child and the adopters whose feelings are involved but a variety of birth family members. Everyone concerned will experience powerful emotions about this, often far from spontaneous, relationship. It is important for adopters to bring their strengths and self-confidence to the task and not to allow negative thoughts to predominate.

Thoughts and feelings about the birth family will predominate at certain times:

- telling the adoption story;

- letterbox exchanges;

- face-to-face contact with birth family members;

- an adopted child asking about or searching for birth relatives.

Telling the adoption story

One adopter found this difficult and wondered why.

It makes me feel so strange. I ask myself why do I find it so hard, and I think it's because telling her reminds me of my own loss, as well as Ann's loss of her birth parents. It helps so much that we met Ann's mother. In reality she is not a threat. (McMillan and Irving, 1999, p. 7)

Many adoptive children have difficult birth stories which call for skill and sensitivity in the telling. It is natural for their adoptive parents to feel protective towards them and to experience some anger that they have to face such unpleasant truths about their origins. This is one situation amongst many when infertile adopters can draw strength from their own experience. Morrison suggests that letting an adoptive child know about the sadness of infertility can be helpful to the child:

It may help your child both to know that, like him or her, you understand that things do not always work out as you might have planned or hoped, and also that if you face up to that, other ways forward can be found. (2007, p. 154)

"Letterbox" exchanges

Virtually all adopters nowadays are expected to provide an annual report on their child for birth relatives via the agency's "letterbox" and, if possible, to receive an annual report from birth parents in return. This is again something with which biological parents do not have to contend and can be a reminder of the "unfairness" of it all, especially if a request from a birth parent for news and information comes out of the blue after some years of silence. When it works well, adoptive parents will have the satisfaction of feeling they have helped birth relatives to cope with their loss a little better and created openings for their children to follow up on their own in the future.

Face-to-face contact

Some adopted children benefit from more direct forms of contact with either birth parents or other birth family members, e.g. grandparents or a sibling. This is a challenging task for any adopter and can be stressful for the child or young person. Happily, it can sometimes result in warm relationships and a sense that everyone's family life has been enhanced.

Neil and Howe (2004, pp. 31–2) list the characteristics of all three parties to contact which will help or hinder the success of a contact plan. In adopters, they are, like Walker (2008), looking for adults in a secure/autonomous state of mind, sensitive and capable of showing empathy towards a birth relative, with a reflective capacity and an ability to communicate well in social situations. They warn against unresolved feelings relating to attachment, loss or abuse.

Just as at the beginning of an adoption journey, infertile applicants crave control over their own lives and the adoption processes in which they have had to become involved, similarly Logan and Smith (2004) found that:

> Contact worked best where adoptive parents and birth relatives were well prepared and were involved in detailed planning for contact arrangements. (p. 121)

Neil (2004) notes that it helped when:

> Everybody had a clear sense that it was adoptive parents who had ultimate control over contact arrangements . . . From the adopters' perspective, this sense of control reduced anxieties. From the birth relatives' point of view, boundaries are very clear. (p. 82)

Adopted adults' search for birth relatives

Over the last quarter century, many birth parents and other relatives have been traced and many adoptive parents and their adult children have struggled to accommodate the new reality in their relationship. Inevitably, adopters have wondered whether they would still feel like parents to their children and many children have avoided potential pain for their parents and confusion for themselves by conducting the search in secret, or postponing it until after their adopters' death. Trinder *et al* (2005) emphasise that all the evidence from the adoptees themselves suggests that, whatever the strength of the new relationship, their adopters who brought them up remain their "parents". This should assuage the acute anxiety that many adopters, perhaps particularly infertile adopters, can feel when a previously unknown parent forges an emotional tie with their child. They did find, however, that 'it [the adoptee's search] can sometimes bring to the surface old and deep feelings of not being the "real" parent' (p. 83), feelings to which infertile adopters may be especially vulnerable.

The child in the adoptive family

All the aspects of bringing up an adopted child which are the subject of matching discussions become, thereafter, the stuff of everyday life for the adopters and their child. No parent ever manages to fulfil all their own initial aspirations for family life but adopters who lack self-esteem as a result of their infertility can be particularly susceptible to feeling that they are letting their child and themselves down. By contrast, some of those who may have appeared less willing to share the emotions associated with their infertility with their assessing social worker during a home study may nonetheless prove to be dynamic and supportive parents once they have a child placed with them. An experienced social worker observes:

> For those who . . . longed to be a parent, I still find it strangely fascinating the way people open up after a placement. The stress of the process and pain is visibly removed from their faces. They look more relaxed, happy and grow in confidence in the months after placement. It is one of the continuing delights of the job. They are the ones who turn up smiling at the Christmas party and are always willing to talk to others in the process who want to know what it's like to adopt. (Personal communication)

There is no benefit to anybody if adopters waver in their sense of entitlement to be their children's parents. It is this sense which, when accompanied by love and a growing attachment, provides children with feelings of security and permanence. It is important, therefore, for adopters to be strong enough to nurture an enduring sense of belonging in their family. This is a task with many dimensions and below we touch on just three of these:

- accepting the child for him/herself;
- dealing with the consequences of early trauma;
- parting company.

Accepting the child for him/herself

The same social worker notes:

Those who can "let go" of the intense pain of infertility and move forward to adoption by the overriding desire to be a parent, can open their minds better to parenting that child who is not born to them. These adoptions will be more positive and successful, the adopted child can find their own place in the family, for the birth/fantasy child has been put to rest. (Personal communication)

As the years go by, the genetic differences between parents and children in an adoptive family may be continually underlined and, in adolescence, enhanced. It is critical that children and young people receive affirmation of their parents' love and acceptance of them. If this proves difficult, Reich (1990) emphasises that it is never too late to do "grief work" around feelings associated with infertility and a "fantasy child", though pointing out how much more beneficial it is to have done this work prior to the adoption taking place.

Dealing with the consequences of early trauma

Some adopted children confound the prophets and develop into healthy young people with robust personalities, despite adverse beginnings. Others do not and it is sometimes not easy to predict who will fall into which camp. Committed adopters whose children find life hard usually put huge effort into helping them in whatever way they can, including making use of their experiences of infertility:

They will put their all into helping their child make that attachment and overcome their problems. Making sense of their own loss helps here. They are open and can relate to the child's grief and sense of loss over their own little lives.

They share the child's loss with them rather than rush to cover it all up, make it all better because that shields them from their own pain. I always counsel couples to let a sad or grieving child cry, comfort them, be with them and understand them. This helps the child to build trust, recover and move on. It also helps create a bond between them. (Personal communication)

She also notes that:

. . . they are also the ones who will be determined to seek post-adoption support, there is no shame or fear of failure. (Personal communication)

This sense of inadequacy and failure is something a child with difficulties can easily re-ignite. It is tragic if this feeling comes to dominate, as it will adversely affect the parent–child relationship and may also deter the adopters from seeking and making good use of vital post-adoption support and services. Reich (1990) suggests that an agency which keeps in touch with its adopters post-placement may be able to help them by anticipating that old wounds, including emotions resulting from infertility, may re-open, verbalising this possibility and thus normalising the experience. For the same reason, she recommends that agencies automatically offer a service to adopters when their children are in the pre-adolescent phase.

Parting company but staying together

Most adopted young people leave home when they have reached appropriate maturity and with their adopters' blessing but, sadly, there will be times when adoptive children and their parents cannot live together and the parting is premature. If this happens while the children are still young enough to be found new parents, adopters may be able to withdraw in a careful, planned way to minimise further damage to the child. They will be very distressed that their own dreams of family life have come to this and pain and anger from the experience will be resurrected. A disruption meeting can do something to alleviate such feelings and adopters should also be informed about counselling opportunities which they may take up at a later date.

More usual is the situation where an older child or teenager finds themselves in crisis and unable to live peaceably with their adoptive family. If adoptive parents are still vulnerable to revisiting past feelings of failure associated with infertility, they may collapse at this very moment when they need to be strong. Instead, they should approach their local agency to access appropriate post-adoption and other services to help themselves and their child weather the storm.

Quite often, young people re-enter public care at this point, if only on a temporary basis. It should still be possible for young people to leave home in a planned way that protects them until they have gained greater maturity, e.g. by moving to a foster home or supported lodgings. This is the moment for adopters to be reminded that the adoption order conferred lifelong parenthood. They should be helped to hold on to their sense of entitlement to be their child's parents, however strongly the young person may be rejecting them, and the local authority which has accommodated the child should act in a way that respects and fosters this. Research has shown that many adopted young people are able to reforge relationships with their adopters when they have gained additional maturity. Howe writes:

In most cases the anger and hostility of these preoccupied and agitated children seemed finally to blow itself out . . . If parents managed to "stay with" their "angry" son or daughter through adolescence and beyond, often they experienced not only a more relaxed relationship, but in some instances a particularly affectionate one. It was as if their now grown-up child had finally accepted, at a barely conscious level, that they really were loved and wanted. (1996, p. 104)

If their adopters withdraw, reconnecting with the old feelings of failure stemming from their infertility and feeling no longer fit to be their parents, the young person is vulnerable to being effectively without parents at all at a stage in life when they still desperately need them.

ISSUES AND TASKS FOR SOCIAL WORKERS

- **Prepare infertile adopters for feelings of grief, failure and inadequacy which might be reawakened down the years.**

- **Help adopters to utilise the strengths gained from their experience of infertility.**

- **Make sure that adopters know how to access post-placement and post-adoption support from the agency and other sources.**

- **Stress the importance of the adopters holding on to a sense of entitlement to be their child's parent, even if the child is in serious trouble, is rejecting, or leaves home prematurely.**

KEY MESSAGES

- **Infertility's "aftershocks" can continue to affect adopters for many years.**

- **Adopters can use their experience of infertility to help their child cope with sadness and trauma.**

- **Adopters need help in bringing up their children and to maintain their confidence in themselves as parents.**

Conclusion

The original idea of writing this guide stemmed from several sources. These included the writers' own experience of working with infertile adopters over years, the supervision of assessing social workers, and perhaps primarily involvement in a number of adoption panels, both as members and as Chair. Overall, this left us with a clear conviction of the significance and relevance of infertility to the task of adoption and yet it seemed as if the subject was not always adequately confronted or even understood by either the applicant or the worker at the various stages of the adoption process.

For the person who has always presumed that there will be children some day, a diagnosis of infertility is likely to have a profound effect. For many, this will be the most devastating blow which life has dealt to date and both they and their social worker need to recognise it as the starting point on the road to becoming a parent by adoption. Along the way, they will have experienced a range of powerful, fluctuating emotions of varying intensity and these need to have been managed and regulated, at least to the point where they are unlikely to impede the individual in parenting an adopted child over the years.

Every individual will respond differently to what they have undergone in relation to infertility, and what they are about to experience in adoption. As one observer comments:

> Other common reactions [i.e. other than pain, grief and a sense of bereavement] are irritation, sadness, confusion, embarrassment, fear, courage, closeness to a partner, a feeling of profound intrusion and eventually boredom with the whole sorry process. (Personal communication)

We have attempted to highlight the relevance of these reactions and experiences to adoption at all stages, including post-approval and in the years following the granting of the adoption order.

To an extent, all adopters are likely to face some of the same issues, as parents to a child not born to them. It would be overly simplistic to claim that infertility was the reason behind every adopter's response to every given circumstance. Nevertheless, there will be situations where infertile adopters'

experiences may prove of particular value in caring for their child or, conversely, may leave them potentially more vulnerable and exposed and in need of specific support. For assessing social workers, keeping in mind the infertility issues that we have outlined in this guide will help to improve the adoption experience for all infertile adopters.

Bibliography

Archer, C. and Gordon, C. (2006) *New Families, Old Scripts: A guide to the language of trauma and attachment in adoptive families*, London: Jessica Kingsley Publishers.

Ashton, L. (2008) *Take Two: A story of baby adoptions*, London: BAAF.

Barker, S., Byrne, S., Morrison, M. and Spencer, M. (1999) *Making Good Assessments*, London: BAAF.

Beesley, P., Hutchison, B., Millar, I. and de Sousa, S. with Fursland, E. (2006) *Preparing to Adopt*, London: BAAF.

Bentley, S. (2008) *The Guardian 16.02.08, Family Supplement*, p. 3.

Bingley Miller, L. (2005) *Adoption: Issues for infertility counsellors*, Sheffield: British Infertility Counselling Association (BICA).

Black, R. and Scull, L. (2005) *Beyond Childlessness*, London: Rodale.

Brebner, C., Sharp, J. and Stone, F. (1985) *The Role of Infertility in Adoption*, London: BAAF.

Brodzinsky, D., Smith, D. and Brodzinsky, A. (1998) *Children's Adjustment to Adoption: Developmental and clinical issues*, Thousand Oaks, CA: Sage.

Cousins, J. and Morrison, M. (2003) *Right from the Start: Best practice in adoption planning for babies and other children*, London: BAAF.

Cowling, S. (undated) *Aspects of Adoption no.1: Adoptive families*, London: Post-Adoption Centre.

Greene, S., Kelly, R., Nixon, E., Kelly, G., Borska, Z. and Murphy, S. (2007) *A Study of Intercountry Adoption Outcomes in Ireland*, Dublin: Children's Resources Centre/Adoption Board.

Howe, D. (1996) *Adopters on Adoption*, London: BAAF.

Irwin Johnson, P. (1992) *Adopting after Infertility*, New York, NY: Perspectives Press.

James, M. (2006) *An Adoption Diary*, London: BAAF.

Logan, J. and Smith, C. (2004) 'Direct post-adoption contact: experiences of birth and adoptive families', in Neil, E. and Howe, D. (eds) *Contact in Adoption and Permanent Foster Care*, London: BAAF, pp. 105–123.

Lowe, N. and Murch, M. (1999) *Supporting Adoption*, London: BAAF.

McMillan, R. and Irving, G. (1999) *More than Love*, Edinburgh: Stationery Office.

Main, M., Hesse, E. and Goldwyn, R. (2008) 'Studying differences in language usage in recounting attachment history', in Steele, H. and Steele, M. (eds) *Clinical Applications of the Adult Attachment Interview*, New York and London: Guilford Press, pp. 31–68.

Mallon, G. and Betts, B. (2005) *Recruiting, Assessing and Supporting Lesbian and Gay Carers and Adopters*, London: BAAF.

May, P. (2005) *Approaching Fatherhood: A guide for adoptive dads and others*, London: BAAF.

Morrison, M. (2007) *Talking about Adoption to your Adopted Child*, London: BAAF.

Neil, E. (2004) 'The "Contact after Adoption" study: face-to-face contact', in Neil, E. and Howe, D. (eds) *Contact in Adoption and Permanent Foster Care: Research, theory and practice*, London: BAAF, pp. 65–84.

Neil, E. and Howe, D. (eds) (2004) *Contact in Adoption and Permanent Foster Care: Research, theory and practice*, London: BAAF.

Office for National Statistics (ONS) (2008) *Marriage, Divorce and Adoption Statistics: Review of the Registrar General on marriages and divorces in 2005 and adoptions in 2006, in England and Wales*, London: ONS.

Owen, M. (1999) *Novices, Old Hands and Professionals*, London: BAAF.

Rawlings, D. and Looi, K. (2007) 'Yes, men want children too', *BICA Journal of Fertility Counselling*, 14:1, pp. 23–28.

Reich, D. (1990) *Preparing People to Adopt Babies and Young Children*, Discussion Paper, London: Post Adoption Centre.

Rockel, J. and Ryburn, M. (1988) *Adoption Today: Change and choice in New Zealand*, Auckland: Heinemann Reed.

Trinder, L., Feast, J. and Howe, D. (2005) *The Adoption Reunion Handbook*, London: John Wiley.

Walker J (2008) 'The use of attachment theory in adoption and fostering', in *Adoption & Fostering*, 32:1, pp. 49–57.

Winnicott, D. (1964) *The Child, the Family and the Outside World*, Harmondsworth: Pelican.

Useful organisations

British Association for Adoption and Fostering
Head Office
Saffron House
6–10 Kirby Street
London
EC1N 8TS
Tel: 020 7421 2600
www.baaf.org.uk

Southern England
As above
Tel: 020 7421 2671

Central and Northern England
Unit 4, Pavilion Business Park
Royds Hall Road
Wortley
Leeds
LS12 6AJ
Tel: 0113 289 1101

Cymru
7 Cleeve House
Lambourne Crescent
Cardiff
CF14 5GP
Tel: 029 2076 1155

Scotland
40 Shandwick Place
Edinburgh
EH2 4RT
Tel: 0131 220 4749

Northern Ireland
Botanic House
1–5 Botanic Avenue
Belfast
BT7 1JG
Tel: 028 9031 5494

Adoption UK
46 The Green
South Bar Street
Banbury OX16 9AB
Tel: 01295 752240
www.adoptionuk.org.uk

British Infertility Counselling Association
111 Harley Street
London W1G 6AW
Information line: 01372 451626
www.bica.net

Human Fertilisation and Embryology Authority
21 Bloomsbury Street
London WC1B 3HF
Tel: 020 7291 8200
www.hfea.gov.uk

Infertility Network UK
Charter House
43 St. Leonards Road
Bexhill-on-Sea
East Sussex TN40 1JA
Tel: 0800 008 7464
www.infertilitynetworkuk.com

The Miscarriage Association
c/o Clayton Hospital
Northgate
Wakefield
West Yorkshire WF1 3JS
Helpline: 01924 200799
www.miscarriageassociation.org.uk

APPENDIX 1 Family life cycle tasks of adoptive parents and adopted children

Age Period	Adoptive Parents	Adopted Children
Pre-adoption	Coping with infertility Making an adoption decision Coping with the uncertainty and anxiety related to the placement process Coping with social stigma associated with adoption Developing family and social support for adoption decision	
Infancy	Taking on the identity as adoptive parents Finding appropriate role models and developing realistic expectations regarding adoption Integrating the child into the family and fostering secure attachments Exploring thoughts and feelings about the child's birth family	
Toddlerhood and pre-school years	Beginning the telling process Coping with anxiety and uncertainty regarding the telling process Creating a family atmosphere conducive to open adoption communication	Learning one's adoption story Questioning parents about adoption
Middle childhood	Helping child master the meaning of adoption Helping child cope with adoption loss Validating the child's connection to both adoptive and biological families Fostering a positive view of the birth family Maintaining open communication about adoption	Mastering the meaning of adoption Coping with adoption loss Exploring thoughts and feelings about birth parents and the relinquishment Coping with stigma associated with being adopted Maintaining open communication with parents about adoption Validating one's dual connection to two families
Adolescence	Helping the adolescent cope with ongoing adoption-related loss Fostering positive view of the birth family Supporting the teenager's search interests and plans Helping the adolescent develop realistic expectations regarding searching Maintaining open communication about adoption	Integrating adoption into a stable and secure identity Coping with adoption loss Exploring thoughts and feelings about birth family and birth heritage Exploring feelings about the search process Maintaining open communication with parents about adoption

(This table is reproduced from *Children's Adjustment to Adoption: Developmental and clinical issues*, by David Brodzinsky, Daniel Smith and Anne Brodzinsky, published by Sage Publications, 1998)

APPENDIX 2 Pathways to adoption

Internalised/expressive grieving process

Disbelief:

Shock, denial, numbness at possibility of being infertile/childless.

Searching:

Restlessness, internal longing. Feel sad and unfulfilled.

Anger:

'Why me? What have I/we done to deserve this?'

Guilt:

Blame oneself. My own body has let me/us down.

Depression:

Sense of loss and of hopes and dreams of parenting. Open grieving; tears.

Adjustment:

Begin to accept the loss. Make the best of it. Get involved with nieces and nephews; get pleasure from being with these children. See adoption as a possibility of parenting.

Rehabilitation:

Start to let go of anger and despair. Begin to get excited about adoption process and way forward. Social worker may be presented with enthusiastic/ eager applicants ready to accept all case scenarios. May be easy to identify their grief process and plot progress through it, but need to be sure they could empathise with a child's loss and not be overwhelmed by their own joy.

Acceptance:

Integration of loss. Can easily project themselves into adoptive parenting. Enthusiasm comes through, as it was never dampened down – they have always accepted feelings of powerlessness in life. Referees crucial in helping social worker understand that couple/person is realistically focusing on adoption and not just "parenthood". Offers here may be unrealistically wide, need to pin offer to their strengths, not just their wishes.

Externalised/defensive grieving process

Dismissive:

It'll happen one day. Put thoughts of parenthood to one side.

Refocus:

Find other ways of gaining fulfillment and achieving in life.

Resentment:

Aimed at others with children. 'It's not fair: it's easy for them'.

Defiance:

Dismiss parenthood. 'What's so great about it anyway?'

Determination:

Put up barriers to protect against pain and feelings of sadness. May avoid getting experience of children. Get on with career but begin to consider adoption as a way of achieving parenthood.

Resignation:

Begin adoption process with feelings of powerlessness. Social worker may be presented with defensive stance. 'This is what I must go through to reach my goal. Others don't have to.' Grief process harder for social worker to identify. May have to look for signs of empathy towards others as a way of seeing how they might relate to a child.

Acceptance:

Work with the assessment, albeit finding it hard to be in a disempowered relationship. Joy of adoption may not be revealed until placement. Referees crucial here to learn more about the inner emotional capacity of this person(s). The open, more relaxed side of their personality may be harder to find. Offer may be mainly 'would discuss'. Need to be able to identify their strengths through their defences.

(Reproduced with kind permission from Jackie Quick, Norfolk County Council)

APPENDIX 3 Susan's infertility diary 1998–2006

Date	Event	Details
July 1998	Bought first house together	Andrew and I bought our first and only house together. This was very exciting for us, we still love living in the house now which is in a lovely area close to shops and parks.
April 1999	Married	One of the happiest days of my life, marrying in the church where my parents and grandparents had been married: where I had been to Sunday School and where my grandfather is buried. I also changed my name (outside of work) to Andrew's.
September 2002	Finding out that we would not be able to have children naturally	This was a very distressing occasion. Andrew had previously undergone tests to eliminate any reason why he could not father children before I underwent very painful and invasive tests. The doctor misread Andrew's results, telling him there were no significant problems. After the emotionally draining day we were told by the consultant that we would never be able to have children naturally and the only option was IVF. Andrew and I were very upset at the results. I remember having to go on a residential course with work and not wanting to leave Andrew and him not wanting me to go. The staff at the clinic were very insensitive and unsympathetic which contributed to the stress of the treatment throughout our time at this clinic.
January 2003	First full IVF treatment (first clinic)	Due to my age (34) the clinic fast-tracked us for our first course of treatment. I did find the treatment very hard, due in part to my fear of needles and my nervousness following the pain of my tests. I was ill during the first IVF treatment, vomiting and choking, which I know distressed Andrew as he was in the theatre with me. I did try to be optimistic but was not surprised that the treatment did not work first time.
July–December 2003	First frozen IVF treatment	I was not surprised that this treatment did not work.
December 2003	Second full IVF treatment	I took some of my annual leave to try and ensure that I had the best chance of making this treatment work. Unfortunately the clinic changed their mind about when I should go up to it for egg collection, which resulted in me swelling up due to the drugs which caused me additional stress and it upset Andrew to see me in pain and discomfort.
January–August 2004	Preparation for and third IVF treatment (new clinic)	I decided to try everything I could to ensure that this treatment would work. I started acupuncture (which was brave, given my fear of needles), continued with reflexology, gave up caffeine and alcohol and started an organic and largely dairy-free diet. When the treatment did not work, I was a lot more upset this time as I felt it would never work.

Date	Event	Details
June–November 2005	Three frozen IVF treatments	We delayed having any more frozen IVF treatments until we had the results of a number of tests which the clinic said would find out if there was any reason why the previous treatments had not worked. These were invasive and painful and, unfortunately, inconclusive. After the failure of the frozen cycle in June, I decided to work part-time and try to lose weight (the side effect of the IVF treatment was that I had put on three stone in weight). We had two further treatments in October/November, neither of which was successful.
December 2005	Decided to stop any future IVF treatment and adopt our family	We decided after much discussion that after seven failed IVF treatments, that it was unlikely to work and that we had tried our best. We also agreed that we still wanted a family and wanted that to be through adoption. I called the local adoption centre and was told by the social worker that we would have to wait until six months after the last failed IVF treatment before commencing the adoption process.
January 2006	Decided to have fun!	After deciding to adopt our family and also feeling that IVF had taken over our lives for the previous three years, we decided to make the most of being childless whilst waiting for our family to come along. As a couple we have had the most amazing time which has involved trips to exotic places all over the world.
September 2006	Information meeting	Attended information meeting to begin the adoption process.

(Personal communication, reproduced with kind permission from the author)

APPENDIX 4 Exercises

EXERCISE 1

Consider the following questions individually and then share and compare with your partner (if you are in a relationship).

1. What does being a mum mean?

2. What does being a dad mean?

3. What messages do people receive from our society about having children?

4. List reasons why you think people have children.

5. Which of these reasons particularly apply to you?

EXERCISE 2

Patricia Johnston, an adoptive parent, identified six main areas of loss that she thinks people must have thought about before entering into adoption. She suggests that prospective adopters need to assess themselves in relation to these losses. This process can also be used to work out where some extra support may be needed or where an individual may need to pay attention to themselves, (or a partner, or together as a couple), at any stage in the adoption process, including after placement. Adopters could also re-visit it from time to time and see what changes have taken place. Below is a table based on these ideas.

1. Consider the following question: "If I had had the power to avoid personally experiencing one or more of these losses, which would I have chosen to avoid? – i.e. which are the most significant losses to me and which are the least?"

2. Rank the statements from 1 to 6 with number 1 being the most significant loss to you and number 6 the least.

3. Next, look at each loss and give it a weighting on a scale of 0 to 3 according to the following:

   0   experiencing the finality of this loss means little or nothing to me;

   1   this loss bothers me somewhat, but other losses bother me more;

   2   this loss is relatively important for me;

   3   experiencing this loss is very painful for me.

	Ranking 1–6	Weighting 0–3
Loss of control over many aspects of your life.		
Loss of individual genetic continuity linking past and future.		
Loss of a jointly conceived child with your life partner.		
Loss of the physical experience of pregnancy, (including getting your partner pregnant, if a man), birth and early infancy.		
Loss of the emotional experience of pregnancy, (including getting your partner pregnant, if a man), birth and early infancy.		
Loss of the opportunity to parent.		

(This table is reproduced from *Sexuality and Fertility Issues in Ill Health and Disability: From early adolescence to adulthood*, by Rachel Balen and Marilyn Crawshaw, published by Jessica Kingsley Publishers, 2006)

EXERCISE 3

Think about yourself as "the person I am today".

- What has had a positive influence on your identity and self-esteem?
- What has left you feeling less self-assured and/or undervalued?
- How might these factors affect you when you become an adoptive parent?
- What three things worry you most about becoming a parent by adoption?
- What three things do you look forward to most about being a parent?

CHECKLIST FOR ASSESSING WORKERS

- Do you know what this couple's fertility impairment means to them now? As individuals and as a couple?
- Do you know what effect their infertility investigations and treatment had on them?
- Do you know what being a biological parent means to them now? As individuals and as a couple?
- Do you know what being an adoptive parent means to them now? As individuals and as a couple?
- Do you know what coping strategies they have as individuals and as a couple for managing difficult situations?
- Do you have a sense of what infertility-related stresses they might have to manage as adoptive parents? What external help have they already accessed? What extra help might they need from social workers, as individuals and as a couple?

(This checklist is reproduced from *Sexuality and Fertility Issues in Ill Health and Disability: From early adolescence to adulthood*, by Rachel Balen and Marilyn Crawshaw, published by Jessica Kingsley Publishers, 2006)